D0999922

tapas

tapas

a taste of spain in america
josé andrés

with richard wolffe

Clarkson Potter / Publishers
New York

Copyright © 2005 by José Andrés
All rights reserved.

Published in the United States by Clarkson Potter/Publishers, an imprint of
the Crown Publishing Group, a division of Random House, Inc., New York.
www.clarksonpotter.com

CLARKSON N. POTTER is a trademark and POTTER and colophon are
registered trademarks of Random House, Inc.

Library of Congress Cataloging-in-Publication Data
Andrés, José,
Tapas: a taste of Spain in America / José Andrés; with Richard Wolffe.—
1st ed. Includes bibliographical references and index.   1. Tapas—United
States.   2. Cookery, Spanish.   I. Wolffe, Richard.   II. Title.
TX740.A6854   2005
641.8'12—dc22   2004027466

ISBN 1-4000-5359-5

Printed in China

Photographs by Francesc Guillamet
Design by Tasty Concepts
Art Direction by Roberto Sablayrolles

1 2 3 4 5 6 7 8 9 10

FIRST EDITION

To our half-oranges: Tichi and Paula.
And our little gnomes in the mushroom fields:
Carlota, Ines, Lucia, Ilana, Ben, and Max.

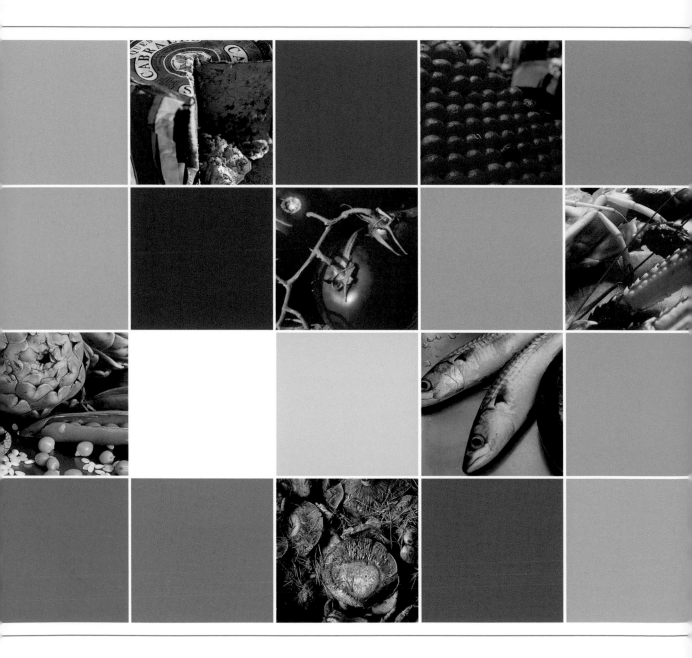

contents
contenido

preface
prefacio

I arrived on these shores twelve years ago as a young Spaniard who thought he knew it all. What I discovered was not the end of my journey, but the start of one. For the last decade and more, I've been searching inside myself for the meaning of Spanish cooking. Searching for the traditional cooking I grew up with, and adore, and live for. To me, it's so much more than work or what pays my salary. It's a way of life. I smell, I breathe, I think, I dream of cooking—and, more often than not, of Spanish cooking. As I've traveled across America, I've learned so much about this country's cooking and so much more about my own country's cooking. I'm absorbed by the search for what happened through the centuries—the different cultures, religions, and peoples that shaped Spanish cooking into what it is today. It was only by exploring the New World that I could see the real nature of the Old.

Every night at my tapas restaurants, we try to bring the culture and the flavors of Spain to America. Yet for me, something else happened while I was re-creating the best of my country: by bringing Spanish cooking to America, I discovered how to combine traditional Spanish dishes with the amazing ingredients and bounty of this extraordinary country. I don't import fish from Spain for all our dishes (sometimes it even comes from the Pacific Ocean) But that doesn't mean that my Spanish cooking is any less traditional or less authentic in America. On the contrary: it becomes richer by adapting its spirit to the flesh of the local ingredients. I could spend days telling you how great things are in Spain: the fish, the meat, the soul of the country. But after spending half my adult life in the United States, I have grown into a unique hybrid, combining the best traditions I learned at home with the open-minded approach that lies at the heart of America.

My first contact with the United States was as a young sailor in the Spanish navy, visiting Pensacola, Norfolk, and New York. I thought at the time that I had accomplished my childhood dream of visiting the United States. But somewhere on that trip, something inside me told me I'd be coming back. A few months later, after returning to Spain, I finished my military service and flew back to New York—this time as a *cocinero,* or cook. All I had was a small bag on my back, a couple of chef's coats, a little money, and a big dream of conquering America with Spanish cooking. I was also lucky enough to have a job at two restaurants: El Dorado Petit and Paradis Barcelona. El Dorado Petit was one of the best restaurants in Spain, and it was trying to sell New York its version of Catalan cooking. Unfortunately, neither restaurant made it.

Even though they lost a lot of money, those restaurants did an amazing job of trying to refresh what Spanish restaurants should be (and showed me, as a young chef, some critical mistakes). During my time in New York, one person who influenced me more than anyone else was Clemente Bocos, at El Cid in lower Manhattan, an amazing little tapas place. Clemente became like a father to me, with a ready phrase to guide me and a deep interest in my future. One very cold night, while we were sharing the most wonderful garlic soup and I was venting my frustrations about the restaurants, Clemente gave me a very wise piece of advice: "José," he said, "no matter what you do, don't try to reinvent Spanish cooking in America. Don't try to guess what Americans would like to eat. Cook what you remember from Spain. Don't listen to people who say, 'They won't like this or that.' If you stick to the basics, and execute them well, people will like your cooking, and they will like Spanish food."

That was just before I was contacted by my current partners and friends, Roberto Álvarez and Rob Wilder, who told me they wanted to open a tapas place in Washington, D.C., and needed a

Spanish chef. They gave me the restaurants, and I gave them my expertise, my ideas, and my spirit. The lessons I'd learned in New York proved invaluable in creating Jaleo—a catchy name for a Spanish restaurant, named after the John Singer Sargent painting of a flamenco party. Eleven years later, the woman at the heart of this classic painting now dances on the walls of three Jaleos, each serving 5,000 people a week.

I can't tell you how many of our friends and customers at Jaleo started coming to the restaurant as children and have brought their first dates to Jaleo. It makes me smile inside to know that, at least in Washington, a younger generation has grown up knowing and understanding the cooking of my land. It's been hard work, and we still have a long way to go, but Spanish food is more widely available than ever, and Spanish wines are better known than ever. And I think the best is still to come.

This book is a celebration of the two countries that are closest to my heart; of the best that Spain and America have given me; of my love for the food, the ingredients, and the people that make it happen. I hope you'll find your own reason to keep exploring Spanish food, and to keep making it happen in America.

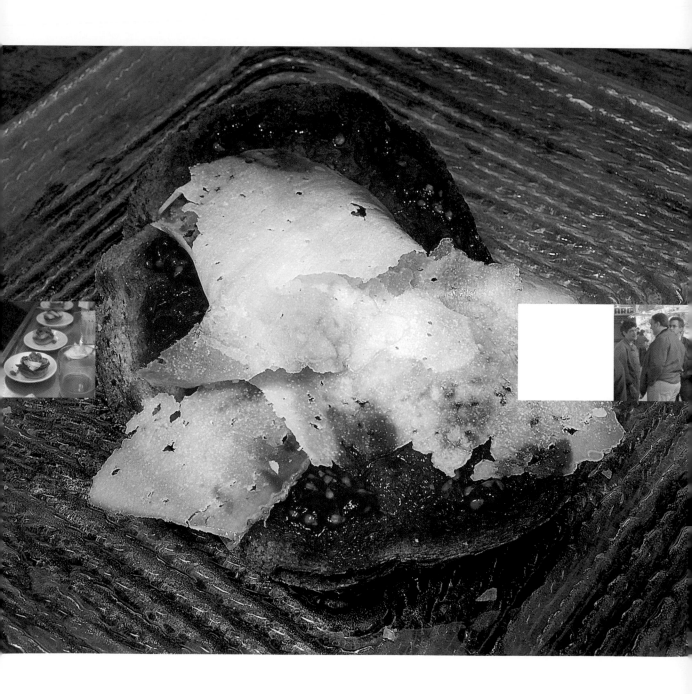

introduction
how to use *tapas*

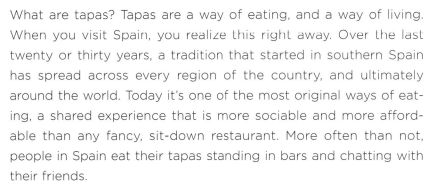

What are tapas? Tapas are a way of eating, and a way of living. When you visit Spain, you realize this right away. Over the last twenty or thirty years, a tradition that started in southern Spain has spread across every region of the country, and ultimately around the world. Today it's one of the most original ways of eating, a shared experience that is more sociable and more affordable than any fancy, sit-down restaurant. More often than not, people in Spain eat their tapas standing in bars and chatting with their friends.

You may have heard stories about how tapas started out as something to cover a glass of wine in taverns. The word *tapa* means lid, and the idea is that the food (perhaps a slice of ham) was used to protect a drink from flies or other foreign objects. Yet there are no historical accounts or records of any such thing. Many people think this story is just a myth, even if it's been widely repeated over time. What we do know is that tapas are a part of Mediterranean culture, not so different from Greek and Turkish *mezze* or the multiple dishes at a Moroccan feast.

Initially tapas were just a few olives, anchovies, or mussels on a small plate. But they've ended up being almost anything served in small portions. In the Basque country, they're called *pinchos*, after the toothpick that holds them together. The most famous is called Gilda, after the Rita Hayworth movie of the 1940s: an olive, a guindilla sweet pepper in vinegar, and a marinated anchovy, all held together by a toothpick. More commonly, *pinchos* rest on a small round slice of bread. When you walk into a bar like Bergara in a town like San Sebastián, you'll find platters of *pinchos*—of foie gras with mango, and mushrooms in seafood sauce—sitting on the countertops, waiting for you to help yourself.

For me, tapas are something to share and mix. There are no rigid rules about separating meat and chicken, fish and vegetables. There are no appetizers and entrees. You can build a whole meal around a series of dishes that you like. You'll find egg dishes that are perfect for brunch, salads that are great for a summer lunch, and meats that are perfect for dinner. Or you could just as easily eat the salads for brunch, the meats at lunch, and the eggs for dinner. Try mixing dishes according to your taste. With tapas, the eating and sharing are just as important as the food you're serving. And if you like the tapa and don't want to make other small dishes, you can easily double the quantities in these recipes to make an entree for four people.

To help select your tapas, this book is organized by ingredient, like cheese, eggs, onions, potatoes. They're all foods you can find at your local supermarket. Some ingredients are particular to Spanish cooking, like the sweet, smoky paprika called *pimentón,* which gives our chorizo sausages such a wonderfully intense flavor. For these few Spanish specialties, there's a list of suppliers at the back of the book.

Since I arrived in the United States, Spanish food has become more widely distributed than ever. You can find real Manchego cheese in Safeway and real wood-roasted piquillo peppers in Whole Foods or Wegmans. *Jamón serrano,* our dry-cured ham, is one of the best in the world and worth seeking out from a specialist. Spanish meat producers have perfected the curing technique better than anyone else, and even our more affordable hams are superior to their international rivals. As for Spanish olive oil, it's the essence of Spanish cooking. Just as Spanish wine reflects the authentic flavor of the land and climate of Spain, our olive oil is rooted in Spanish tradition and is at the heart of many of the tapas you'll find here.

Spanish wines are themselves becoming more and more widely available. With each tapa, I've recommended a wine, including its area of origin in Spain and the grape variety. From the classic red Tempranillo grape (used in Rioja and Ribera del Duero) to the Alvariño white grape, Spanish wines have an incredible range and versatility, which are great to explore alongside the recipes in this book. And don't forget the exquisite sherry wines, which remain underappreciated by the wider world.

There was a time when many Italian foods were hard to find and Moroccan couscous was an exotic rarity. Now you can find them everywhere, and I believe that many Spanish ingredients will soon find their rightful place on the shelves of American supermarkets across the country. In the meantime, my first suggestion is to buy plenty of extra-virgin olive oil (a Spanish one, of course). You'll be using a lot of it in these dishes.

This book is aimed at the home cook, not the professional, because tapas are for eating at home or with friends. It doesn't demand special expertise, even if there are techniques that might seem a little new. And it doesn't require any expensive equipment, although you might consider investing in good candy and meat thermometers, as well as a mortar and pestle (if you don't already have them). I hope you enjoy exploring Spanish food, and enjoy the life of tapas. *Buen provecho!*

olives and olive oil

chapter 1

Recipes	Wine tips
Allioli a la Catalana Traditional garlic and oil sauce	Barbara Fores Blanc from the Terra Alta region (Garnacha Blanca/Viognier grapes)
Allioli a la moderna Modern garlic and oil sauce	Fino "La Ina" from the Jerez region (Palomino grape)
Aceitunas aliñadas al aceite de oliva, naranja y tomillo Olives marinated in orange and thyme-infused olive oil	Palacio de Menade from the Rueda region (Sauvignon Blanc grape)
Setas salvajes marinadas Confit of wild mushrooms	Jean Leon from the Penedes region (Chardonnay grape)
Aceitunas verdes rellenas de pimiento y anchoa Green olives filled with piquillo peppers and anchovy	Manzanilla "La Gitana" from the Jerez region (Palomino grape)
Ostras con aceitunas y alcaparras al limón Oysters with olives, capers, and lemon	1+1=3 Cava Brut from the Cava region (Xarelo/Macabeo/Parellada grapes)
Pan con chocolate, aceite y sal Rustic bread with dark chocolate, olive oil, and salt	Oloroso Dulce "Matusalem" from the Jerez region (Pedro Ximénez grape)
Pulpo a feira "Lincoln copper penny" Octopus with olive oil, pimentón, potato, and a copper penny	Luna Beberide Bierzo from the Bierzo region (Mencia grape)

aceitunas y aceite de oliva

As you drive through the Spanish countryside in November and December, you can see men shaking long sticks into the trees. They scoop up their haul in big plastic sheets on the ground and empty them carefully into deep crates that are stacked at the side of the road. It's an unglamorous start to one of the most essential ingredients in Spanish cooking: olive oil. The olive harvest is a magical time, when hard black and green olives are transformed into liquid gold. You only have to walk into a pressing room to experience the alchemy of it: the warm wet space is like a steam bath of olive oil that infuses the air, your face, and the entire room.

You might think that what emerges is the same across Spain and southern Europe. It's not. Spanish olive oil is much like a fine wine. Its uniqueness comes from the different olive varieties, and the different soils and climates they grow in. For far too long, olive oil has been used as a one-dimensional ingredient with labels telling you only which country it's from. This doesn't tell the whole story. For instance, the Catalan region in the north produces fruitier oils that are perfect for salad dressings, while the southern regions produce a more robust oil that is slightly bitter and is better suited for gazpacho. Then there are the different olives, such as Arbequina (which is slightly fruity and is great drizzled over bread that's been rubbed with tomato) and Picual (which tends to be more woody and is great for frying).

Since the Phoenicians first planted olive trees on the Iberian peninsula, olive oil has been the king of Spanish cooking. In fact olive oil is used so widely and so boldly in Spain that it's no exaggeration to say that we have more olive oil–based recipes than any other country in the world. Olive oil can be used in very simple ways, such as drizzling it over cheese. Or you can use it to sear fish or shellfish *a la plancha*—on a flat griddle top—where the oil acts as a thin film between the food and the metal. It's also the main ingredient in dressings, acting as an emulsifier in gazpacho or in mayonnaise. Then there's the olive oil bath: you can submerge just about anything in very hot olive oil to deep-fry it, and you just have to taste a *cro-*

queta to know that Spain (and especially Andalucia) is the center of the frying world. Of course you can always pan-fry, and nothing is more comforting than an egg that has been pan-fried in olive oil. But you can also use oil as you use water: poaching a piece of fish or vegetable in oil at a very low temperature allows you to capture its inner moistness. Olive oil even entered the world of iced desserts when the Adrià brothers invented the olive oil sorbet.

In Spain we have several traditional olive oil dishes that deserve much more attention from the rest of the world. Among them is *alli-oli,* which is made by smashing a few cloves of garlic into a paste in a traditional mortar. Olive oil is then added very slowly, drop by drop, with a continuous circular movement of the pestle, until you have a very dense, thick sauce. I've learned many traditional sauces from many different parts of the world, but *allioli* in the Catalan style is one of the most amazing ones because it challenges the basic laws of physics, turning the liquid oil into a solid form with a little garlic and a lot of work.

That's why we call it liquid gold. It might look like just another bottle of olive oil, but inside there's a trove of new techniques, new dishes, and new flavors.

Traditional garlic and oil sauce

Makes about 1 cup

4 garlic cloves, peeled

1 pinch of salt

½ teaspoon fresh lemon juice (from about ¼ lemon)

1½ cups Spanish extra-virgin olive oil

Allioli is an incredibly popular and versatile sauce that is eaten all across Spain with fish, meat, and vegetables. This recipe is the real thing: *allioli* the old-fashioned way, made with a mortar and pestle. In the Catalan countryside, you can still find a few restaurants that go to the trouble of making *allioli* this way. It's perfect on top of the grilled meats and sausages that are at the heart of Catalan cooking. But it's not just the taste that makes this sauce so incredible—it's the process. It's hard to believe that olive oil and garlic can come together to create something so rich and buttery. It may take a bit of work, but a little goes a long way.

Place the garlic in a mortar and add the pinch of salt. Using the pestle, smash the garlic cloves to make a smooth paste. (The salt stops the garlic from slipping at the bottom of the mortar as you pound it down.)

Add the lemon juice to the garlic. Then, drop by drop, add the olive oil as you continue to crush the paste with the pestle. Keep turning the pestle with a slow, continuous circular motion around the mortar as you drip the oil in slowly and steadily. Make sure the paste soaks up the olive oil as you go. Keep adding the oil drop by drop until the sauce has the consistency of a very thick mayonnaise. If your *allioli* gets too dense, add ½ teaspoon water to thin it out. This process takes time—around 20 minutes of slow motion around the mortar—to create a dense, rich sauce.

José's tips

It's hard to think, when you start crushing the garlic, that it will ever turn into something as dense and smooth as *allioli*. But don't give up. It's really worth the time and effort to see the oil and garlic come together. Just make sure you're adding the olive oil slowly, drop by drop. Keep moving the pestle around the mortar in a circular motion. And keep dreaming of the thick, creamy sauce you'll have at the end of it all.

 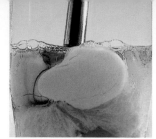 

Allioli a la moderna
Modern garlic and oil sauce

Makes 1 cup

1 small egg

1 cup Spanish
extra-virgin olive oil

1 garlic clove, peeled

1 teaspoon sherry vinegar
or fresh lemon juice

Salt to taste

Not everyone has the time to make *allioli* the traditional way, by hand, even though it's worth the effort. This is the modern version, made with a hand blender, in case you're rushed.

Break the egg into a small mixing bowl. Add 2 tablespoons of the olive oil, the garlic clove, and the vinegar or lemon juice.

Using a hand-held electric mixer, mix at high speed until the garlic is fully pureed into a loose paste. Then, little by little, add the remaining olive oil as you continue blending at high speed. If the mixture appears too thick when you begin adding the oil, add 1 teaspoon water to loosen the sauce. Continue adding the oil and blending until you have a rich, creamy *allioli*. The sauce will be a lovely yellow color. Add salt to taste.

José's tips

What happens if the oil and egg separate? Don't throw the sauce out. You can do two things: One is to whisk it and use it as a side sauce for fish or a vegetable. Or if you want to rescue the *allioli*, measure out 1 tablespoon lukewarm water and add it to the mix little by little. Blend it again until you have the creamy sauce you wanted.

Aceitunas aliñadas al aceite de oliva, naranja y tomillo

Olives marinated in orange and thyme-infused olive oil

Serves 4

1 orange

1 lemon

4 garlic cloves, peeled

¼ cup Spanish extra-virgin olive oil

2 tablespoons sherry vinegar

2 sprigs fresh thyme

½ teaspoon salt

½ pound olives (your own favorite variety or mixture)

In the markets and bars of Spain, you find olives everywhere. After all, Spain is the biggest producer of olives in the world. But what makes each olive really distinctive is the *aliño*, the mixture of spices and other flavorings that gives the olives their taste. In southern Spain some people buy their olives fresh and cure them for several days before marinating them in their favorite *aliño*. But you can buy your favorite cured olives and marinate them in your own *aliño* to create something richer and tastier than a storebought marinated version. This one has a bright citrus flavor that is offset by the subtle accent of the thyme.

Using a vegetable peeler, remove one quarter of the zest from the orange and lemon and set aside. Cut the orange in half and juice it. Split open the garlic cloves by placing them on a chopping board and pressing down hard on them with the base of your hand or with the flat side of a knife. In a large bowl, combine the orange and lemon zest with the orange juice, garlic, oil, vinegar, thyme, and salt. Add the olives and mix well. (An easy way to do this is to combine the olives and the dressing in a plastic container with a lid and simply shake.) Marinate for at least 12 hours, covered, and serve at room temperature.

José's tips

For the fullest flavor, let the olives marinate at room temperature for a week before serving.

Setas salvajes marinadas
Confit of wild mushrooms

Makes 1¹/₂ cups

10 pearl onions

3 ripe tomatoes

2 cups Spanish extra-virgin olive oil

1 pound mixed fresh wild mushrooms (chanterelles, morels, hedgehogs), cleaned

3 cloves

1 teaspoon black peppercorns

1 teaspoon salt

4 sprigs fresh thyme

2 tablespoons sherry vinegar

In Spain we've been making *conservas*—what the French call *confits*—with olive oil for centuries, usually with meats and fish. You can also make them with all kinds of vegetables, and I love mushrooms the most. The texture and flavor of the mushrooms become more intense in the confit process. Today the best *conservas* in Spain, sold in cans and jars at high prices, are considered to be some of the country's finest cuisine—a far cry from their original function as a way of preserving perishable food and staving off winter hunger.

Place the onions in a bowl of hot water for 4 minutes to make them easier to peel. Using a paring knife, cut off a little of the round root end of each onion and carefully peel away the outer leathery skin. Set the onions aside. Cut each tomato in half lengthwise. Place a grater over a bowl and grate the open side of the tomato into the bowl. Strain the grated flesh through a sieve to produce 1 cup of tomato puree.

In a large saucepan, heat 2 tablespoons of the olive oil over a medium flame. Add the onions and cook until they turn a light brown color, about 3 minutes. Add the tomato puree and cook until the mixture reduces to a thick, dark red sauce, about 10 minutes.

Add the rest of the oil and the mushrooms. Mix in the cloves, peppercorns, and salt. Stir the mushrooms a few times, being careful not to break them apart. Raise the heat to medium-high and continue cooking until the olive oil starts to bubble slightly, at around 160 degrees (measured with a candy thermometer). As soon as you see the first bubbles, remove the pan from the heat and pour the contents into a serving bowl. Place the thyme on top, pushing the sprigs into the oil to release the aroma.

Allow to cool to room temperature. Then stir in the vinegar, and serve immediately.

José's tips
By allowing the mixture to cool at the end, you're able to maintain the fresh flavor of the vinegar.
   If you can't find wild mushrooms, use shiitake or oyster mushrooms instead.

Aceitunas verdes rellenas de pimiento y anchoa
Green olives filled with piquillo peppers and anchovy

Serves 4

8 extra-large green olives, unpitted (see tips)

4 anchovy fillets (oil-packed)

2 piquillo peppers (Spanish wood-roasted sweet peppers)

1 garlic clove, unpeeled

3 tablespoons Spanish extra-virgin olive oil

Grated zest of $\frac{1}{2}$ orange

1 tablespoon sherry vinegar

Sea salt to taste

There's no better tapa than a good stuffed olive. But the ones you usually find in the supermarket are filled with poor-quality pepper and even poorer anchovy. One of the best appetizers for a lunch or dinner is to take a good olive and stuff it with the real thing. Simple ingredients prepared in a simple way—that's the best way to take your everyday cooking to a higher level.

Using the flat side of a knife, press each olive until the pit pops out, being careful not to split the olive in half. Cut the anchovy fillets lengthwise to create 8 long slices, and cut the piquillo peppers into eight $\frac{1}{2}$-inch-wide strips.

Place 1 anchovy slice and 1 pepper strip in each olive. You can be generous with the filling, allowing the anchovy and pepper to spill out of the olive.

Split open the garlic clove by placing it on a chopping board and pressing down hard with the base of your hand or with the flat side of a knife. In a small bowl, mix the garlic, olive oil, orange zest, and vinegar. Place the stuffed olives in the dressing and allow them to marinate for 30 minutes. Then sprinkle with a little sea salt and arrange them on a plate, with toothpicks for serving.

José's tips

Buy unpitted olives for this dish. It's more work for you, but the olives are usually better quality and have meatier flesh.

Piquillo peppers come in 8-ounce (or larger) jars. They are available at specialty markets and on the Internet (see Sources, page 250).

Ostras con aceitunas y alcaparras al limón
Oysters with olives, capers, and lemon

Serves 4

8 Malpeque oysters (or any other fresh oyster)

1 lemon

4 manzanilla olives, pitted and finely chopped

1 tablespoon small capers (packed in brine)

1 tablespoon finely chopped shallot (about 1 small shallot)

1 tablespoon Spanish extra-virgin olive oil

1 tablespoon fresh lemon juice (from about ½ lemon)

Grated zest of ¼ lemon

1 tablespoon finely chopped chives

I'm the biggest oyster eater in the world. Every year, I can't wait for Oyster Week at two of my favorite D.C. restaurants—The Old Ebbitt Grill and Kinkead's. They have some of the best oysters I've ever eaten: the unique American tiny Olympias and the salty Kumamotos. (Don't tell anyone, but I wait until mid-afternoon, when the Old Ebbitt serves its oysters at half-price. That way I get to eat twice as much.) Spaniards believe they have the best shellfish in the world, but North American oysters are something irresistible. This recipe is unbelievably popular at my restaurants, and one of my favorites for guests at home.

Bring 1 quart of water to a boil in a large pot. Add the oysters and boil until you see them opening just a fraction, 15 to 20 seconds, depending on the size.

Drain the oysters and place them in a strainer set over a bowl. Open the oysters: Hold an oyster in a towel. Insert the blade of an oyster knife into the "hinge" at the back of the shell. Twist the blade until the hinge pops. Using a small sharp knife, cut upward to sever the muscle that opens and closes the shell. Now carefully insert the knife underneath the oyster to release it from the shell. Be careful not to break the oyster itself. Remove the membrane around the oyster and discard it. Make sure you do this over the bowl so you catch all the juices the oyster releases. Set aside the oysters and the juices.

Cut the ends off the lemon and sit it on a flat surface. Cutting vertically, trim away the skin and pith of half the lemon to expose the flesh. Then slice along the sides of 2 segments and pull out the flesh. Cut each segment into 4 small pieces. Set aside

In a small bowl, mix together the olives, capers, shallot, olive oil, lemon juice, and half the lemon zest. Add the oyster juices and mix together.

Make a bed of the olive mixture on a small plate and place the oysters on top. Place 1 small piece of lemon flesh on top of each oyster. Sprinkle with the chives and the remaining lemon zest. Serve immediately.

José's tips

You can leave the oyster membrane, as it's traditionally served, but I find the membrane has a bitter taste that diminishes the sweet and pristine flavor of the oyster. If you like oysters, I can only imagine how much you'll love the taste of oysters prepared this way. They really taste like the pearls of the sea.

Rustic bread with dark chocolate, olive oil, and salt

Serves 4

4 ½-inch-thick slices
rustic bread (see tips)

4 ounces dark chocolate

4 tablespoons Spanish
extra-virgin olive oil

Sea salt to taste

I don't want to be chauvinistic here, but Spaniards are the people who brought cocoa beans back to Europe. By the eighteenth century, the royalty and the aristocracy of Spain were drinking chocolate sweetened with sugar all day long. Chocolate bars as we know them today would come later from central Europe. Spaniards will always have a sweet tooth for chocolate, and this simple dessert is one of the best examples of that—a uniquely Spanish mix of olive oil and chocolate on bread.

Heat the oven to 200 degrees.

Toast the slices of bread in a toaster until brown. Using a knife, break the chocolate into small pieces. Scatter them over the toasted bread, and place in the oven until the chocolate melts, about 5 minutes.

Drizzle with the olive oil, sprinkle a little salt on top, and serve.

José's tips

Make sure you use a good country bread with a thick crust and a light interior, full of holes—not a dense sourdough. The chocolate itself is a matter of taste: some prefer it bitter, others like it sweet and milky. Experiment with your favorite chocolate.

Pulpo a Feira "Lincoln copper penny"
Octopus with olive oil, pimentón, potato, and a copper penny

Serves 4

2 tablespoons salt

1 clean copper penny

1 bay leaf

1 tablespoon black peppercorns

1 whole octopus (about 2 pounds)

4 small potatoes, such as Yukon Gold, peeled

¼ cup Spanish extra-virgin olive oil

Sea salt to taste

½ teaspoon *pimentón* (Spanish sweet paprika)

This dish is also called *Pulpo a la Gallega* because it's traditional in the Galicia region, where at special celebrations you can still see people cooking hundreds of octopus in big copper cauldrons at bars and restaurants. The copper adds a characteristic red color to the octopus. Here we may not have the big copper pots, but by adding a penny we can recreate some of the old magic.

Bring 4 quarts of water to a boil in a large pot. Add the salt, copper penny, bay leaf, and peppercorns. Grab the octopus by the head and dunk it three times just below the head (without scalding yourself!) in the boiling water. Then place the whole octopus in the water and lower the heat to a simmer. Cook uncovered for 1¼ hours.

Add the potatoes and cook for another 15 minutes, or until the octopus is tender. You can test for doneness by inserting a toothpick in the thickest part of the tentacle, just as you would with a cake. The toothpick should easily pierce the octopus, with little resistance. Use tongs to remove the octopus and the potatoes from the pot, and set them aside.

Cut the tentacles off the octopus and discard the head. Cut the tentacles into ½-inch pieces.

Slice the potatoes and arrange them in a serving dish. Place the octopus on top. Drizzle with the olive oil and season liberally with sea salt. Place the *pimentón* in a fine-mesh sieve, and tapping the side of the sieve gently to break up any large chunks, sprinkle it evenly over the top. Serve with toothpicks.

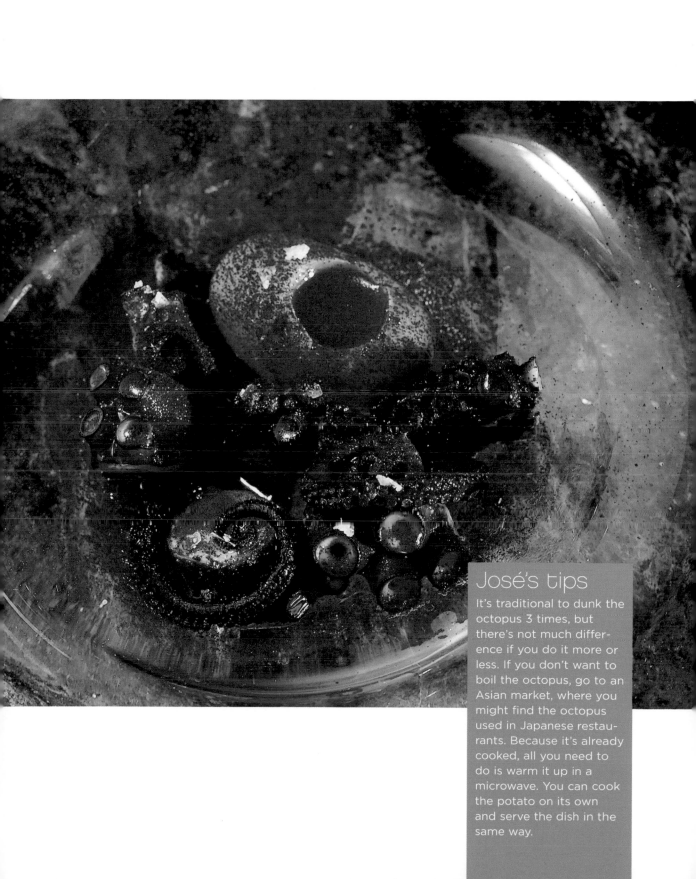

José's tips

It's traditional to dunk the octopus 3 times, but there's not much difference if you do it more or less. If you don't want to boil the octopus, go to an Asian market, where you might find the octopus used in Japanese restaurants. Because it's already cooked, all you need to do is warm it up in a microwave. You can cook the potato on its own and serve the dish in the same way.

tomatoes

chapter 2
capitulo 2

tomates

Every summer I travel to Pennsylvania to visit a farm for its latest produce, especially its almost endless array of tomatoes. Green Zebras, Purple Cherokees, Striped Germans, Brandywines: the names are as tantalizing and varied as their flavors. But the farm behind them, the Tuscarora co-op, is just as extraordinary. Tuscarora was set up by Jim and Moie Kimball Crawford, the owners of New Morning Farm, the largest organic farm in the state. At New Morning, which lies in a picturesque crescent between a small creek and the hills above, the Crawfords grow small-scale crops like sweet young corn, crisp lettuce, flavorful garlic, and the juiciest, tastiest tomatoes. Jim and Moie wanted to do something more than grow their own organic food, however; they wanted to help other small organic farmers, among them Pennsylvania's famous Amish farmers, who face huge obstacles in sending their produce to the big cities. By establishing the co-op and helping those smaller farmers, Jim helped everyone in the area by dramatically expanding the range of food we can buy—especially heirloom tomatoes, grown from original American seeds, which have such individual tastes and characters.

It's fascinating to use these American tomatoes to create Spanish dishes. After all, the introduction of New World tomatoes to the Old World created the single greatest change in Mediterranean cooking. Who could imagine Mediterranean cuisine today without *sofrito*, a sauce of sautéed onions and fresh tomatoes—the basis for a thousand dishes across the region? In fact the first published recipe for tomatoes in the Old World is in a seventeenth-century Italian book that describes a "Spanish-style" tomato sauce. Nowadays it's hard to think of Spanish cuisine without gazpacho, the best-known cold soup in the world, which mixes New World tomatoes with Old World garlic, olive oil, and sherry vinegar. Tomatoes have given Spanish cooking an extraordinary range and versatility—in soups, salads, stews, and sautéed dishes.

Among the recipes here, you'll see instances where we use different parts of the tomato separately. The texture, taste, and look of tomato seeds are so different from the tomato flesh. It's worth taking

the trouble to prepare them separately, to transform salads into something special.

In Spain we use mainly plum tomatoes, which are widely available here. But it's also worth experimenting with different American varieties in various Spanish dishes. Try a yellow heirloom in gazpacho, or even a shocking Green Zebra (your brain tells you the green tomato isn't ripe, but it's as sweet as they come). Experiment with a peachy Brandywine in a salad, or a smoky Purple Cherokee to add subtle richness to your sofrito. It might not be as dramatic as the arrival of the first tomatoes in Europe, but there are still plenty of surprises and innovations that the New World can bring to the Old.

Pan con tomate y jamón serrano
Tomato toast with Spanish ham

Serves 4

4 slices rustic bread

2 ripe tomatoes

Spanish extra-virgin olive oil,
for drizzling

Salt to taste

4 thin slices *jamón serrano*
(Spanish cured ham)

This is quite simply a classic. In many ways, it's the national dish of Catalonia, where you'll find it at the start of any good tapas meal—in homes, bars, and restaurants. There's something deeply satisfying, even comforting, about the combination of warm bread, ripe tomato, and golden oil. You can top it with anchovies or cheese instead of ham if you like. Here are two versions of the dish: In the first, more traditional recipe, we rub the tomato directly on the bread, and the crunchiness of the toast acts like a grater. In the second, we use a grater, mixing the tomatoes with olive oil and salt. The grater works well if you are preparing this dish for a party.

The traditional way

Toast the bread. Set aside.

Cut the tomatoes in half. Rub the open face of the tomatoes into one side of each piece of toast until all the flesh is grated. Throw the skin away.

Drizzle olive oil, as liberally as you like, over the tomato. Season with salt to taste.

Place a slice of ham on top. Drizzle with a little oil again. Serve.

The modern way

Cut the tomatoes in half. Place a grater over a large mixing bowl. Rub the open face of the tomatoes into the grater until all the flesh is grated. Discard the skin.

Add 3 tablespoons of olive oil to the grated tomato in the bowl. Season with salt to taste.

Toast the bread.

Spoon the tomato mixture over the slices of toast. Place a slice of ham on top of each. Drizzle with a little more oil, and serve.

José's tips
If you're having a barbecue over the summer, try roasting your bread over the charcoal. You'll make the best tomato toast ever.

Sofrito
Catalan tomato and onion sauce

Makes 3 cups

10 ripe plum tomatoes

1½ cups Spanish extra-virgin olive oil

4 small Spanish onions, peeled and finely chopped (about 4 cups)

1 teaspoon sugar

1 teaspoon salt

1 teaspoon *pimentón* (Spanish sweet paprika)

1 bay leaf

Sofrito is the sauce that launched a thousand dishes. It's the essence, the foundation, of Spanish cooking. This meeting of the Old World of olive oil and the New World of tomato makes the perfect basis for any starring ingredient—chicken, fish, shellfish. You'll use this recipe again and again in tapas cooking. Master it, commit it to memory, and open the door to Spain.

Cut the tomatoes in half. Place a grater over a large mixing bowl. Rub the open face of the tomatoes over the grater until all the flesh is grated. Discard the skin.

Heat the oil in a medium saucepan over a medium-low flame. Add the onions, the sugar, and the salt. Cook, stirring occasionally with a wooden spoon, until the onions become soft and tender and turn a light brown color, about 45 minutes. You want the onions to caramelize. If they get too dark, add ½ tablespoon of water to keep them from burning while they cook.

Add the reserved tomato puree, the *pimentón,* and the bay leaf. Cook for another 20 minutes over medium heat. You'll know your sofrito is ready when the tomato has broken down and deepened in color, and the oil has separated from the sauce.

José's tips

The key to this sauce is the onion, not the tomato. Make sure the onion is cooked well enough that it's soft and sweet—sweet enough to smell—before you add the tomato. Then use your judgment with the seasoning, including the sugar.

You can make this sauce several days in advance and store it in an airtight container in the refrigerator. You'll use it time and again to great effect.

Gazpacho al estilo de Tichi
Tichi's Gazpacho

Serves 4

For the gazpacho

2 pounds ripe tomatoes
(about 10 plum tomatoes)

½ pound cucumber
(about 1 cucumber)

3 ounces green bell pepper
(about ½ bell pepper)

1 garlic clove, peeled

2 tablespoons sherry vinegar

¾ cup Spanish
extra-virgin olive oil

2 teaspoons salt

For the garnish

3 tablespoons Spanish
extra-virgin olive oil

1 slice rustic white bread

8 plum tomatoes, with the
seeds prepared as "fillets"
(see page 40)

12 cherry tomatoes, halved

1 cucumber, peeled and cut
into ½-inch cubes

4 pearl onions, quartered and
pulled apart into segments

1 tablespoon sherry vinegar

Sea salt to taste

4 chives, cut into
1-inch-long pieces

My wife, Patricia (aka Tichi), is from Andalucia, a region known for its sherry and its hams. But not many people know that Andalucia is the cold-soup capital of the world, thanks to gazpacho. Every summer, when you open the refrigerator in my house, you'll see a big glass pitcher full of this rich, creamy red liquid. It's always ready to refresh you on a hot day. My wife doesn't like to cook, and she always tries hard to change the menu at home. But one thing she cooks like the gods is gazpacho. This is her recipe. It's also one of the reasons I married her.

Cut out and discard the core at the top of the tomatoes, and chop the tomatoes roughly into quarters. Place in a blender. Peel the cucumber and cut it into chunks. Add them to the blender. Cut the bell pepper in half, and remove and discard the core and the seeds. Chop the pepper into large pieces and place them in the blender. Add the garlic, sherry vinegar, and ½ cup of water, and blend until the mixture becomes a thick liquid. The red tomatoes will have turned a wonderful pink color. Taste for acidity (this will vary with the sweetness of the tomatoes). If it's not balanced enough, add a little more vinegar. Add the olive oil and salt. Reblend. Then pour the gazpacho through a strainer into a pitcher. Place it in the fridge to cool for at least 30 minutes.

While the gazpacho is chilling, prepare the croutons: Heat 1 tablespoon of the olive oil in a small pan over a medium-high flame and fry the bread until golden on both sides, about 2 minutes. Break the bread into small pieces to form 16 croutons, and set aside.

When you are ready to serve the gazpacho, place 4 croutons, 2 "fillets" of tomato seeds, 6 cherry tomato halves, 3 cucumber cubes, and 3 onion segments in each bowl. Add a few drops of the remaining olive oil to each onion segment, and drizzle a little more oil around the bowl. Add a few drops of vinegar to each cucumber cube, and drizzle a little more around the bowl. Sprinkle sea salt on the tomatoes, and sprinkle the chives over all. Pour the chilled gazpacho over the garnish, at the table.

José's tips

If you want to be original, buy yellow or even green tomatoes. You'll surprise your guests.

If you want to save time, you can simplify the garnish immensely: just use a few cubes of cucumber, tomato, and green pepper.

Ensalada de tomates con vinagreta de Jerez y hierbas frescas al Cabrales

Tomato salad with sherry vinegar, fresh herbs, and blue cheese

Serves 4

8 cherry tomatoes

2 pounds ripe tomatoes

2 tablespoons Spanish extra-virgin olive oil

½ tablespoon sherry vinegar

Salt to taste

Black pepper to taste

2 tablespoons each of: flat parsley leaves, torn into pieces; chopped chives; chervil leaves, whole; fennel leaves, torn into pieces; dill leaves, torn into pieces

2 pearl onions, peeled and cut into thin slices

¼ pound soft blue Cabrales cheese (or any other good blue cheese, such as Stilton), broken into small pieces

In many Spanish dishes, tomatoes are the backdrop to the starring ingredient—a shellfish or meat. But that doesn't do justice to their flavors and vitality. It takes a simple salad to put the tomato in the spotlight, where you can really see its depth and subtlety in detail. This salad showcases the tomato in all its glory, separating the rich, meaty flesh from the smooth, pulpy seeds. With a few simple techniques, you can transform a familiar tomato into a unique tapa.

Bring 1 quart of water to a boil in a small saucepan. Prepare a medium bowl of ice water, and place it near the stove. Drop the cherry tomatoes into the boiling water and blanch for 10 seconds. Drain immediately and then immerse the tomatoes in the ice water to halt the cooking process. When they have cooled, remove the skins and cut them in half.

Using a sharp knife, slice off the top and bottom of each of the larger tomatoes. Locate the fleshy dividing wall of one segment inside the tomato. Slice alongside the dividing wall and open up the flesh of the tomato to expose the seeds. Remove the seeds and their pulp by slicing around the core of the tomato. Set the seeds aside. Your aim is to keep the pulp of the seeds together to create tomato-seed "fillets" that are separate from the firmer tomato flesh. Repeat with each segment of the tomato.

Remove the tomato skin from the flesh with a sharp knife. Cut the flesh into small cubes. Set aside.

In a small bowl, mix the oil and vinegar together to make a dressing. Season to taste with salt and pepper.

In another small bowl, mix together the parsley, chives, chervil, fennel leaves, and dill.

For each serving, place some tomato cubes in a bowl. Add 2 sets of the pulpy seeds. Then arrange 6 onion slices and 4 cherry tomato halves in the bowl. Place 6 pieces of cheese close to the onions. Pour the dressing on top, and sprinkle with the mixed herbs.

José's tips

This may seem a difficult technique the first time you try it. But once you've practiced a little, you'll be amazed at the range of the humble tomato. This salad works best with a mixture of ripe organic tomatoes. Some tomatoes will have big pulpy seeds; others have none. You'll need to experiment with different varieties to figure out how many seed "fillets" you can extract from each tomato.

Pinchitos de tomate con sandia "Ferran Adrià"
Tomato and watermelon skewers "Ferran Adrià"

Serves 4

8 plum tomatoes, with the seeds prepared as "fillets" (see page 40), discard remainder of tomatoes

¼ seedless watermelon, peeled and cut into eight 2-inch cubes

1 tablespoon fresh lemon juice

1 teaspoon grated lemon zest

¼ cup Spanish extra-virgin olive oil

1 tablespoon sherry vinegar

Sea salt to taste

Fresh herbs or herb flowers (such as lavender or borage), optional, for garnish

Today Ferran Adrià is known as the most complex, avant-garde chef in the world—a Salvador Dalí of cuisine, as the *New York Times* put it. But to me, he's all that and more. Ferran has helped a whole generation of younger chefs to think the unthinkable and to dream up dishes that were once impossible. I was lucky enough to work with Ferran at his landmark restaurant el Bulli in Rosas, Spain. The truth is that, more often than not, Ferran innovates by simplifying dishes, not by making them more intricate. That's the philosophy behind this tapa—a skewer of tomato and watermelon—which Ferran dreamt up a decade ago. It's simple, refreshing, and perfectly balanced between the acidity of the tomatoes and the sweetness of the watermelon.

Take a bamboo skewer and place a tomato-seed fillet on it. Then place a watermelon cube onto the skewer. Repeat with the remaining seven skewers.

In a small bowl, mix the lemon juice, half the lemon zest, the oil, and the vinegar to make the dressing.

Place the skewers on a serving plate and pour the dressing on top. Sprinkle with sea salt, the remaining lemon zest, and the herbs or herb flowers (if using). Serve immediately.

José's tips

Ideally, you should use a microplane for removing the zest of the lemon. If you don't have a microplane, try the very fine holes on a box grater.

If you want to save time, you can use cherry tomatoes instead of the tomato seeds.

Tomatitos rellenos de cangrejo
Crab-filled cherry tomatoes

Serves 4

12 ripe cherry tomatoes

6 hazelnuts, shelled, skinned, and crushed into bits

1/2 teaspoon whole-grain mustard

1/2 teaspoon very finely chopped parsley

2 tablespoons mayonnaise

1 teaspoon Spanish extra-virgin olive oil

1 teaspoon sherry vinegar

3 ounces lump crabmeat, picked over for shells and cartilage

1 teaspoon salt

White pepper to taste

1 large egg, cooked for 10 minutes in simmering water

All around the Mediterranean, it's very common to find vegetables that are stuffed, often with meat, and baked in the oven. This is a great summer version, which is lighter, fresher, and much more modern.

Bring 2 cups of water to a boil in a saucepan. Prepare a small bowl of ice water and place it near the stove. Using a small knife, cut a small X in the bottom of each tomato. Blanch the tomatoes in the boiling water for 3 or 4 seconds. Remove them with a slotted spoon and place them immediately in the ice water to stop the cooking process.

When they have cooled, peel the tomatoes, which should be easy at this stage. Slice off the tops. With the help of a melon scoop or a small spoon, remove and discard the seeds, leaving the hollowed-out tomato flesh.

Toast the crushed hazelnuts in a small sauté pan over medium-low heat, stirring regularly to ensure they don't burn, until they turn light brown, about 3 minutes. Remove them from the pan and set aside.

In a bowl, whisk together the mustard, parsley, mayonnaise, olive oil, sherry vinegar, and the crushed hazelnuts. Add the crabmeat and fold it into the dressing with the salt and pepper. Stuff the hollowed tomatoes with this crabmeat mixture, and arrange them on a serving plate.

Separate the egg white from the yolk of the hard-boiled egg. Holding a small sieve above the stuffed tomatoes, press the egg white through the sieve; you'll get a very fine sprinkle of egg white on top of the tomatoes. Repeat with the egg yolk to produce a yellow sprinkle, and serve.

José's tips

If you find it difficult to do this with cherry tomatoes, use any slightly larger round tomatoes instead.

If you have the time, it's really worth buying fresh crabs and cooking them yourself, as we do in the recipe for Txangurro on page 202.

potatoes

chapter 3

capitulo 3

patatas

Every year the most innovative Spanish chefs gather in a magnificent convention center in the Basque port of San Sebastián. They meet to do something very special: to share and showcase their latest dishes, techniques, and concepts. Where chefs used to keep their best dishes secret, this conference—Lo Mejor de la Gastronomía—is a place where everyone learns from one another. Led by Rafael García Santos, one of our most admired and controversial food critics, it's an inspiring week of new recipes and new ideas.

Yet innovation doesn't come from only what's new or undiscovered. It's also about rediscovering old traditions and making them better. And there's nothing more traditional than *tortilla de patatas,* the classic Spanish omelet that is one of the top dishes in the country. Rafael decided years ago that he wanted to pursue the spirit of the perfect traditional *tortilla,* so he stages a championship among *tortilla* cooks at the conference. The contestants are cooks who serve *tortilla de patatas* every day, using their best eggs, their favorite potatoes, and their particular olive oils. The judges are some of the country's top chefs, who love nothing better than a good *tortilla* for lunch. Many of them have contributed to books paying homage to the *tortilla de patatas,* such as the volume by José Carlos Capel, our other top food critic in Spain. For these critics and chefs, it's more than just a contest over a staple dish. It's a way of preserving and improving the traditions that are the roots of their own culture and innovation.

Tortilla de patatas may be wildly popular now, but potatoes hardly received a warm welcome when they first arrived in Spain in the sixteenth century. Although the Spanish conquistadors mistook them for truffles, the early potatoes were mostly small, bitter, and rumored to be poisonous—like much else from the New World. It was only when monks in Seville began planting them around their monasteries that the humble potato established its popular status— the monks rapidly realized that potatoes were a wonderfully cheap way to feed the hungry, sick, and poor. From such basic needs, the

potato slowly took root in Spanish culture to become a staple of Spanish cooking.

Today the potato is still very much at the heart of both home cooking and the tapas of Spanish bars. Whether it's *tortilla de patatas* or *patatas bravas* (spicy fried potatoes with *allioli*), every family has its own special recipe for the perfectly satisfying potato. Try rediscovering potatoes for yourself with some of the recipes here. And as you do so, experiment with the wonderful variety of American potatoes. Try using Red Bliss for frying *patatas bravas,* Idaho potatoes in purees, and delicious small fingerlings in salads. I've even updated the classic *tortilla* using the best American potato chips. You'll be amazed at how simple and satisfying the combination is.

Mashed potatoes with Torta del Casar cheese

Serves 4

1 pound Idaho potatoes, peeled and cut into chunks

1 1/4 cups heavy cream

3 ounces Torta del Casar cheese (see tips), rind removed, cut into small cubes

1/2 cup Spanish extra-virgin olive oil

1/2 tablespoon salt, plus more to taste

Torta del Casar is a unique and unbelievably creamy cheese from Extremadura, in southwestern Spain. In fact, it's so creamy that it runs at room temperature. Made from sheep's milk, it blends with the potato puree to create a magically smooth and satisfying dish. You may be used to potato pureed with butter; this combination goes far beyond, with the cheese adding an acidic edge to the soft, sweet potatoes.

Bring a large pot of water to a boil, add the potatoes, and boil until soft, about 20 minutes. Drain and pass through a ricer, or mash by hand, to create a smooth puree.

In a small pan, heat the cream to the boiling point. Set aside 1 tablespoon of the hot cream and add the rest to the potatoes. Mix with a wooden spoon until the cream is thoroughly incorporated into the puree. Then vigorously mix in the cheese cubes, using the wooden spoon, until the cheese becomes part of the puree. Little by little, add most of the oil until it too is part of the puree. Stir in the 1/2 tablespoon salt.

Drizzle a little more olive oil and the reserved tablespoon of warm cream over the potatoes. Add more salt to taste, and serve.

José's tips

If you can't find Torta del Casar cheese, you can sometimes find La Serena; or you can even use a very soft Brie. But it's really worth asking a local cheese supplier, or going to an Internet supplier (see Sources, page 250), to track down the real thing.

Patatas bravas
Fried potatoes with allioli and spicy sauce

Serves 4

For the brava sauce

4 ripe tomatoes

2 tablespoons Spanish extra-virgin olive oil

1 teaspoon sugar

1 bay leaf

½ teaspoon *pimentón* (Spanish sweet paprika)

1 pinch cayenne pepper

1 teaspoon sherry vinegar

Salt to taste

For the potatoes

2 cups Spanish extra-virgin olive oil

1 pound Idaho potatoes, peeled and cut into 1-inch cubes

Salt to taste

4 teaspoons Allioli (pages 20 and 22)

1 teaspoon finely chopped chives, optional, for garnish

Patatas bravas is one of those tapas that you'll find in many, many bars. There are hundreds of different recipes for *brava* sauce out there. The traditional dish is a good, crisp potato served with a sauce made with spicy pepper and olive oil; you splash the sauce on top of the fried potatoes. In some places they also serve the potatoes with mayonnaise or *allioli.* In my restaurants in D.C., we serve them with both *allioli* and *brava* sauce, as you'll find here.

Make the *brava* sauce: Cut each tomato in half lengthwise. Place a grater over a bowl and grate the open side of the tomatoes into the bowl. Strain the grated flesh through a sieve to produce 1½ cups of tomato puree.

Pour the olive oil into a small pan and warm it over a low flame. Add the tomato puree, sugar, bay leaf, *pimentón,* and cayenne. Raise the heat to medium and cook until the mixture reduces by one fourth and becomes a deep red color, about 10 minutes. Remove from the heat. Add the vinegar and salt to taste, and reserve.

Prepare the potatoes: Pour the olive oil into a deep saucepan, and heat it to 275 degrees. Place the potatoes in the oil and poach them, frying them slowly until soft, which normally takes between 8 and 10 minutes. The potatoes won't change color but they will soften all the way through. You can test for softness by inserting a toothpick; if it comes out easily, the potatoes are done. Remove them from the pan and drain. Set aside.

Raise the temperature of the olive oil to 350 degrees. Return the potatoes to the pan. Fry until they are crisp and brown, about 6 minutes. Drain, and sprinkle with salt to taste.

Drizzle the *brava* sauce on a serving plate. Top with the potatoes and the *allioli,* and sprinkle with chives (if using). Place some toothpicks on the side of the dish for serving.

José's tips

You can poach the potatoes in advance, then fry them at the high temperature just before you serve them.

Patatas a la Riojana
Potatoes Rioja-style with chorizo

Serves 4

3 tablespoons Spanish extra-virgin olive oil

2 garlic cloves, peeled and chopped

1 small onion, peeled and finely chopped (about 1 cup)

7 ounces chorizo sausage (see tips), cut into ½-inch-thick slices

½ pound Idaho potatoes, peeled and cut into 1-inch cubes

1 teaspoon *pimentón* (Spanish sweet paprika)

1½ teaspoons salt

Paul Bocuse, the godfather of nouvelle cuisine, holds a special place in modern Spanish cooking. Bocuse came to Madrid in the late 1970s to speak at a conference, and his speech inspired a whole movement to revolutionize Spanish cooking, led by Juan Mari Arzak and Pedro Subijana in the Basque country. During his trip, Bocuse famously sampled a plate of *Patatas a la Riojana.* His judgment: it's one of the greatest dishes created by man.

Warm the olive oil over low heat in a large shallow pan. Add the garlic and cook until lightly browned, about 1 minute.

Add the onions and cook, stirring occasionally, until they are soft and tender and have turned a light brown color, at least 20 minutes. You want the onions to caramelize. If they start to get too dark, add ½ tablespoon of water to keep them from burning.

When the onions are caramelized, add the chorizo and continue frying until it too is browned, about 2 minutes. Place the potatoes in the pan and stir to coat them in the oil. Cook for 10 minutes.

Add the *pimentón* and the salt, pour in water to cover, and bring to a boil. Once it reaches a boil, reduce the heat to low and simmer until the potatoes are cooked through and the water has reduced by half, about 20 minutes. You'll end up with a wonderful, thick stew.

José's tips

Look for authentic Spanish chorizo in your local markets or online (see Sources, page 250). After many years, we can finally buy real Spanish chorizo in America, so it's worth locating a specialist supplier to enjoy this uniquely rich and flavorful sausage.

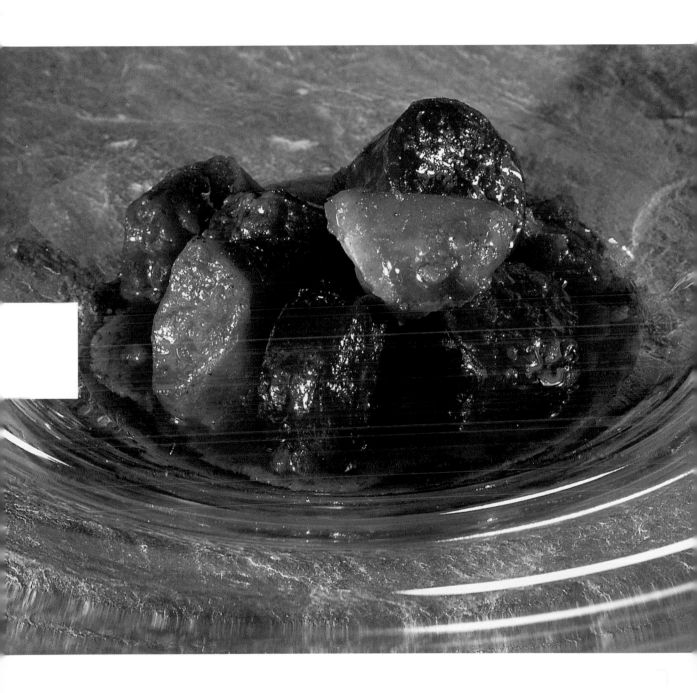

Tortilla de patatas
Potato omelet

Serves 4

2¼ cups Spanish
extra-virgin olive oil

1 pound Idaho potatoes,
peeled, quartered, and
thinly sliced (about 4 cups)

2 teaspoons salt

1 Spanish onion, peeled and
sliced (about 1 cup)

6 large eggs

In any American diner, the heart of a wholesome breakfast is eggs and potatoes. This *tortilla* is built on the same principles: the silken yolk and the soft potato merge in every mouthful. Yet, unlike the eggs at most diners, the magic of the Spanish *tortilla* is its range—from its cooked edge to its creamy interior.

Heat 2 cups of the olive oil in a sauté pan over a medium flame. You'll know the oil is hot enough for frying (275 degrees) when a chunk of potato dropped in the oil jumps a little. Once the oil is hot enough, add the potato slices and fry on both sides until they are lightly browned and the edges are slightly crisp. This should take 10 minutes. Remove the pan from the heat and strain the potatoes, reserving the oil. Season the potatoes with ½ teaspoon of the salt, and set aside.

In another sauté pan, heat all but 3 tablespoons of the reserved potato-cooking oil over a medium-low flame. Add the onion slices and cook until slightly browned, being careful not to burn them, around 8 minutes. Strain the onions and reserve.

Break the eggs into a mixing bowl and whisk them vigorously 3 or 4 times. The eggs should still keep much of their thick, gelatinous consistency. Add the potatoes and onions, plus the remaining 1½ teaspoons of salt, and whisk together. Add the 3 tablespoons of reserved potato-cooking oil to a 6-inch sauté pan, and place over a medium flame. When the oil begins to smoke slightly, add the egg mixture to the pan. As you pour in the eggs, shake the pan vigorously for 10 or 15 seconds to make sure the eggs come together. Then cook for 30 seconds without shaking. Lower the heat and continue to cook for a few minutes. Flip the *tortilla* when the edges are cooked but the center is still wobbly. Place a plate over the pan and invert the pan and plate together so the *tortilla* winds up on the plate, raw side down. If the pan looks dry, add the remaining ¼ cup of fresh oil. Return the *tortilla* to the pan by sliding it back in, raw side down. Continue cooking for another 60 seconds. Serve immediately.

José's tips

You can always use a nonstick sauté pan to make sure your *tortilla* doesn't stick to the bottom. But if you're using a regular pan (preferably one with sloped sides), your *tortilla* won't stick as long as it's hot enough before you add the eggs: watch for the oil to smoke a little before pouring in the eggs. Whatever pan you use, remember to shake it energetically as you start cooking—it's essential for a light *tortilla*. You're aiming for a *tortilla* that is soft and runny inside, but firm and slightly browned on the outside.

Tortilla al estilo Route 11
Route 11 potato chips omelet

Serves 4

7 large eggs

4 ounces good-quality potato chips, such as Route 11's lightly salted chips

2 teaspoons salt

4 tablespoons Spanish extra-virgin olive oil

You might think that using chips—even good-quality, hand-cooked ones —would be a cheap twist on the classic *tortilla de patata*. You'd be wrong. This may be fast and easy (so fast that you can create a wonderfully smooth *tortilla* in just a few minutes), but it's also amazing. Moistening the chips with the egg makes them come alive, as they return to their natural roots with incredible speed. This dish proves that a good *tortilla* is simply egg, potato, and the right frame of mind.

Break 6 of the eggs into a large mixing bowl. Add the chips and stir, crushing them a little as you blend the eggs together. Allow the mixture to sit until the chips absorb a lot of the egg, 5 minutes. Then beat the seventh egg and add it to the egg-chip mixture. Add the salt.

Heat 2 tablespoons of the oil in a small sauté pan (no bigger than 6 inches in diameter) over a medium flame. Add the egg mixture and stir briskly a few times with a wooden spoon to prevent the eggs from sticking to the bottom of the pan. Shake the pan in a circular motion for 10 seconds to keep the mixture loose as the eggs start to stick together. Then lower the temperature and cook for another minute.

Place a plate over the pan and invert the pan and plate together so the *tortilla* winds up on the plate, raw side down. If the pan looks dry, add the remaining 2 tablespoons oil. Return the *tortilla* to the pan by sliding it back in, raw side down. Continue cooking for another 60 seconds. Serve immediately

José's tips

Keep moving the egg mixture in the pan when you first pour it in, or else it will become thick and heavy. You should end up with a perfect *tortilla* in just 3 minutes. This *tortilla* is best enjoyed with runny eggs inside, but if you prefer your eggs less runny, cook it for another minute.

Suquet de peix al estilo de Rafa
Fish and potato stew, Rafa-style

Serves 4

For the picada

4 blanched almonds

1 tablespoon Spanish extra-virgin olive oil

1 slice sourdough bread, crust removed

1 garlic clove, peeled

For the suquet

2 ripe tomatoes

¼ cup Spanish extra-virgin olive oil

2 garlic cloves, peeled and finely chopped

½ pound Idaho potatoes, peeled and cut into 1-inch cubes

½ teaspoon *pimentón* (Spanish sweet paprika)

1 tablespoon chopped parsley

2 cups mineral or filtered water

½ pound monkfish fillet, cut into 4 equal pieces

½ pound rockfish fillet, cut into 4 equal pieces

1½ teaspoons salt

Bread for serving

This is an old, traditional stew that the fishermen make in their boats before returning to port. It's hearty, satisfying, and easy to prepare. *Suquet* starts with a *picada,* a Catalan sauce that is used to add body to fish and meat stews. The *suquet* here is inspired by Rafa, a great eight-table restaurant in the coastal town of Rosas. At Rafa they serve only the fish they catch that day; if they don't catch any good fish, they don't open their doors.

Make the *picada:* Place a small sauté pan over a medium-low flame. Add the almonds, and toast, stirring regularly to ensure they don't burn, until they turn light brown, 3 to 4 minutes. Remove them from the pan and set aside. Add the olive oil to the pan, and once the oil is hot, add the bread and brown it for about 1 minute on each side. Set it aside. Place the garlic clove in a mortar and crush it until you have a thick paste. Add the almonds and crush them into the garlic. Add the bread and continue to crush the mixture together to create your *picada.* Set it aside.

Prepare the *suquet:* Cut each tomato in half lengthwise. Place a grater over a bowl and grate the open side of the tomatoes into the bowl. Strain the grated flesh through a sieve to produce ¾ cup of tomato puree. Set aside. Combine the olive oil and the garlic cloves in a big shallow pan, and cook slowly over medium-low heat, until the garlic starts to look as if it's dancing in the oil, 20 seconds. Add the tomato puree and continue cooking, until it becomes a thick sauce, 5 to 10 minutes. Then add the potatoes and cook for 4 to 5 minutes, stirring the mixture with a wooden spoon.

Sprinkle the *pimentón* and parsley into the pan. Stir for 30 seconds. Pour in the water and stir together. The potatoes should be covered with the mixture at this point. Cook slowly until the potatoes are soft and the sauce is reduced by half, 10 minutes.

Add the fish pieces and the salt. Add the *picada* to the stew, and stir gently to allow its flavor to infuse the mixture. Give the pan a little shake to mix the stew gently. Simmer until the fish is cooked, 3 to 5 minutes. Serve immediately in the pan, with plenty of bread to soak up the delicious sauce.

José's tips

Suquet is also made using a whole snapper (including the bones) cut into 8 pieces. The bones add flavor and intensity to the stew. This stew can also be made with any other meaty fish of your liking.

mushrooms

chapter 4

capitulo 4

Recipes

Sopa de rossinyols al Idiazábal "El Dorado Petit"
Chanterelle soup with Idiazábal cheese

Fricandó de ternera con moixernons
Veal stew with moixernons

Setas en escabeche con jamón
Mushrooms in escabeche with ham

Champiñones al ajillo como hacen en Logroño
White mushrooms with garlic and parsley, as
made in Logroño

Puerros con setas "Clemente Bocos"
Spring leeks with mushrooms

Hongos con patatas
Oven-roasted potatoes and oyster mushrooms

Wine tips

Guitian "Barrel Fermented" from the
Valdeorras region (Godello grape)

Mas de Masos from the Priorat region (Garu-
acha/Carignena/Cabernet Sauvignon grapes)

Bodegas-Hidalgo "Oloroso Viejo Vors" from the
Jerez region (Palomino grape)

Luberri from the Rioja region
(Tempranillo grape)

Gramona III Lustros Brut Natural Gran Reserva
from the Cava region (Xarelo/Macabeo grapes)

Muga "Barrel Fermented" from the Rioja region
(Viura grape)

setas

Nobody loves their mushrooms as much as the Catalans and Basques do. From spring through fall, mushrooms pop up in the northern forests and fields like magic. I remember picking mushrooms in the Pyrenees as a child at summer camp. There, in a field in the middle of nowhere, we would find pounds and pounds of fresh moixernons, a light brown mushroom with a grassy scent, which the camp cook would mix into a meaty stew. It was during those summer camps that we also used to spend our free time catching fresh trout with our bare hands between the rocks of a nearby river. (The trout always put up a good fight, and our fingers were often left raw from the struggle.) Then there were also the rovellò mushrooms we would pick near the pine trees in the Montseny mountains—much bigger and meatier than the moixernon, their rich, woody flavor makes them wonderful grilled, with garlic and parsley.

Today when I'm back in Spain, I don't have to go into the mountains to find such wonderfully fresh mushrooms. I go to my beloved market in Barcelona, la Boquería, where you'll find one of the world's experts on mushrooms, Llorenç Petràs. Many chefs think Petràs has one of the best shops in the market, not least because of the owner's incredible knowledge about wild mushrooms. To Petràs, mushrooms are as mysterious as they are unpredictable—which makes them perfect for creative cooking and new ideas. Just walking past his stall is an experience: at the peak of the season, the aromas are overwhelming. From big cepes to black trumpets, from delicate truffles to wild herbs, a stroll to Petràs is like a walk in the woods. One of my favorite experiences is to sit at the market café Pinotxo to eat the fresh, earthy rovellòs—big brown mushrooms with a distinctive green color under the cap—sautéed with a little oil and sea salt.

Luckily you don't need to go to Barcelona to eat outstanding mushrooms. Today in America you can find dried moixernons, as well as good fresh substitutes like black trumpets, which are delicious stewed. Other mushrooms, like rossinyols (chanterelles) and cepes (porcini), are as widely available here as they are in Spain. And if rovellòs are hard to locate, there are other wonderful varieties like the big and meaty portobellos that are perfect on the grill.

José's tips

If you can't find chanterelles, use any wild mushrooms (one type or a mixture) that are in season. If those are not available, use a farmed variety, such as oyster mushrooms, white mushrooms, or shiitakes.

As for the cheese, if you can't find Idiazábal, use any hard or semi-hard cheese you like, such as Parmesan.

Sopa de rossinyols al Idiazábal "El Dorado Petit"
Chanterelle soup with Idiazábal cheese

Serves 4

1 ounce dried chanterelle mushrooms

½ cup Spanish extra-virgin olive oil

¼ cup shallots (about 2 shallots), peeled and finely chopped

¾ pound fresh chanterelle mushrooms (see tips), cut into small cubes

2 tablespoons dry white wine

1 quart Chicken Stock (page 222)

1 bay leaf

½ cup heavy cream

4 quail egg yolks (or yolks of small chicken eggs)

2 ounces Idiazábal cheese (see tips), finely grated

2 tablespoons finely chopped chives

Sea salt to taste

In the late 1980s El Dorado Petit was the top restaurant in Barcelona, thought by some critics to be one of the best in the world. I worked for the owner, Lluis Cruanyes, when he opened a branch of El Dorado Petit in New York. It was my first job as a cook in the United States, and within a year and a half I was head chef. To this day, Cruanyes remains one of the most influential people in my career—a restaurateur who has a magical presence whenever he steps into the kitchen. This soup, one of his favorites, is brought to life by the Idiazábal cheese—a great smoky sheep's-milk cheese from the Basque country.

Place the dried mushrooms in a bowl, and add just enough warm water to cover. Soak until they are rehydrated, 5 minutes. Strain the mushrooms, reserving 1 cup of the soaking water. Set aside.

Heat ¼ cup of the olive oil in a large saucepan over a low flame. Add the shallots and cook slowly until they are cooked through but not browned, about 10 minutes. Raise the heat to medium and add the fresh mushrooms. Sauté for 3 minutes. If the pan is dry, add a little more of the olive oil. Add the rehydrated mushrooms and cook for 1 more minute.

Pour in the wine and continue to cook over medium heat until it reduces by half, about 30 seconds. Pour in the chicken stock and add the bay leaf. Raise the heat to high and bring to a boil. Once the mixture begins to boil, reduce the heat to low and simmer until the liquid reduces by half, about 10 minutes.

Remove the pan from the heat and mix in the reserved cup of mushroom water and the cream.

To serve, place 1 raw egg yolk in each soup bowl. Sprinkle a layer of cheese around the yolk. Dust the grated cheese with the chopped chives. Sprinkle with sea salt to taste. Serve the soup at the table, ladling it into each bowl on top of the cheese, yolk, and chives.

Fricandó de ternera con moixernons
Veal stew with moixernons

Serves 6

For the picada

10 blanched almonds

2 garlic cloves, peeled

For the fricandó

2 ounces dried moixernon mushrooms (see tips)

½ pound veal scaloppine

½ teaspoon salt

¼ teaspoon black pepper

¼ cup all-purpose flour

¼ cup Spanish extra-virgin olive oil

½ cup Sofrito (page 37)

1 sprig fresh thyme

1 fresh bay leaf

½ cup dry white wine

2 cups mineral or filtered water

José's tips

Today you can find great mushrooms in markets across the U.S.. If you can't find moixernons, which are the traditional mushrooms for this Catalan dish, you can use dried morels, chanterelles, or porcinis.

Fricandó is a classic dish in Catalunya, where both mushrooms and stews are incredibly popular. The first time I made a *fricandó* was when I was studying at the Escola de Restauració i Hostalatge de Barcelona under Josep Puig, the chef at Reno, which was *the* grand, aristocratic restaurant in the city in the 1960s and 1970s. *Fricandó* is the first dish I remember cooking for more than ten people. It tastes as good now as it did when I was just a teenager starting out.

Make the picada: Place a small sauté pan over medium-low heat. Add the almonds and toast, stirring regularly to ensure that they don't burn, until they turn light brown, 3 to 4 minutes. Remove the almonds from the pan and set them aside.

Place the garlic in a mortar and crush it into a paste. Add the almonds and crush them into the garlic. Set aside.

Prepare the fricandó: Place the dried mushrooms in a bowl and cover with lukewarm water. Soak until they are rehydrated, about 5 minutes. Then drain the mushrooms, reserving the water.

Season the veal with the salt and pepper, and coat the pieces on both sides with the flour. Shake the scaloppine a little to remove any excess flour. Heat the olive oil in a medium casserole over a medium flame. When the oil is hot, place 3 or 4 scaloppine in the pan and brown them on each side for around 30 seconds. Don't crowd the pan or the veal won't brown properly. Set the pieces aside, and repeat with the remaining veal. Set aside.

Add the *sofrito* to the pan along with the thyme and bay leaf. Cook over medium heat for 2 or 3 minutes. Then return the veal to the pan and pour in the wine. Simmer until the wine reduces, about 2 minutes. Add the mineral water. Raise the heat and bring to a boil. Once it begins to boil, reduce the heat to low, stir in the reserved *picada,* and simmer until the meat is tender, 30 to 40 minutes.

Remove the tough stalks from the rehydrated mushrooms and add the caps to the stew, along with 1 cup of the reserved mushroom water. Simmer for another 2 to 3 minutes, by which time the sauce should be slightly thick and silky. Serve immediately.

Setas en escabeche con jamón
Mushrooms in escabeche with ham

Serves 6

3 cups Spanish
extra-virgin olive oil

10 garlic cloves

1 sprig fresh rosemary

1 bay leaf

2 sprigs fresh thyme

6 ounces fresh morel
mushrooms, cleaned

1 tablespoon salt,
plus more to taste

1 tablespoon *pimentón*
(Spanish sweet paprika)

¼ cup sherry vinegar

1 tablespoon chopped chives

6 slices *jamón serrano*
(Spanish cured ham)

We Spaniards love our *conservas,* or preserved foods, and we're lucky to have what is probably the best canning industry in the world. Olive oil plays an important role in these canned foods. At home you can make your own *conservas,* without the cans. With the help of olive oil, you can cook meat, fish, and vegetables at a low heat and then store them for a long time. Poaching in olive oil transforms any ingredient. This escabeche is a confit of olive oil and vinegar, and traditionally it's made with sardines or bonito. Here, we use mushrooms and ham for a simple and perfectly balanced tapa.

Heat the olive oil in a medium saucepan over a low flame to 170 degrees (measured with a candy thermometer). Split the garlic cloves open by placing them on a chopping board and pressing down hard with the base of your hand or with the flat side of a knife. Add the split garlic, rosemary, bay leaf, and thyme to the pan, and cook for 5 minutes. Then add the mushrooms, the 1 tablespoon salt, and *pimentón.* Cook, maintaining the temperature at 170 degrees, for 5 minutes.

Remove the pan from the heat and allow to cool. Then add the vinegar and additional salt to taste. The mushroom confit will keep, covered, in the refrigerator for weeks.

When you're ready to serve it, strain the oil from the mushrooms and spoon the confit onto a plate. Sprinkle with the chives and place the ham on top.

José's tips

If the mushrooms are small, this is the perfect tapa to serve with *palillos* (toothpicks). Toothpicks will be the next big thing in America. Believe me, my daughters love them.

Champiñones al ajillo como hacen en Logroño
White mushrooms with garlic and parsley, as made in Logroño

Serves 4

½ cup Spanish extra-virgin olive oil

1 pound white button mushrooms, cleaned

5 garlic cloves, peeled and thinly sliced

1 sprig fresh thyme

¼ cup Spanish manzanilla sherry

Salt to taste

White pepper to taste

1 tablespoon finely chopped parsley

I once visited the heart of La Rioja wine country with my good friends Almudena de Llaguno and Steve Metzer—the couple who pioneered importing Spanish wines to the United States. They took me to a bar in the center of the town of Logroño, where the cooks produced just one dish in their open kitchen: mushrooms with garlic and parsley, served on a small skewer. Their customers face only two choices: how many mushrooms you want on your skewer, and whether to drink red or white wine. Life is tough in La Rioja.

Heat 6 tablespoons of the olive oil in a large sauté pan over a medium flame. Add the mushrooms and leave them in the pan until they brown on one side, 1 minute. Then shake the pan to turn the mushrooms over, and brown again for another minute. Repeat two or three times, until the mushrooms are brown all over. The mushrooms will release some water, but don't worry: if your pan is hot enough, the water will evaporate.

If the pan seems dry, pour in the remaining 2 tablespoons of olive oil. Add the garlic and thyme, and stir with a wooden spoon until the garlic is light brown, about 30 seconds. Be careful not to burn the garlic.

Pour in the sherry and cook until it almost completely evaporates, 1 minute. At this point the pan will contain a nice brown sauce of reduced sherry and mushroom juices. Season with salt and white pepper to taste, sprinkle the parsley on top, and serve immediately in the pan.

José's tips

It's important that the mushrooms are all about the same size to ensure even cooking. If you can only find larger mushrooms, simply quarter them. You can use any meaty mushroom in this dish. Even a portobello, cut into cubes, would be great.

Puerros con setas "Clemente Bocos"
Spring leeks with mushrooms

Serves 4

¹/₂ tablespoon salt, plus more to taste

1 tablespoon black peppercorns

4 large or 8 small leeks, well washed, outer leaves and green part removed

3 tablespoons Spanish extra-virgin olive oil

1 teaspoon Spanish balsamic vinegar

6 ounces oyster mushrooms, cleaned

1 tablespoon chopped chives

When I was young, I would dream of meeting the top chefs of Spain. I bought their books and tried to save up to visit their restaurants. I was lucky: I grew up in the kitchen of Ferran Adrià. When I arrived in New York, I looked for new heroes in America. I began by looking for other Spaniards in America—Julián Serrano, Gabino Sotelino, and Montse Guillén, who made their mark by bringing Spanish cooking to America, and to whom I'll always be indebted. But the one who stays closest to my heart is the late Clemente Bocos, who, with his wife, Yolanda, owned El Cid. Of the many dishes at El Cid (which is still open in New York today), the one that best carries the spirit of Clemente is this simple sauté of leeks and mushrooms. Thanks to dishes like this and people like Clemente, Spanish cooking and tapas have carved a little place in America.

Bring 2 cups of water to a boil in a wide pan, and add the ¹/₂ tablespoon salt and the peppercorns. Add the leeks and simmer slowly until tender, 6 to 10 minutes, depending on their size. Drain, reserving 1 tablespoon of the cooking water.

In a small bowl, mix 2 tablespoons of the olive oil with the balsamic vinegar, the reserved tablespoon of leek-cooking water, and salt to taste. Put the leeks on a dish and drizzle with the dressing.

Pour the remaining 1 tablespoon of olive oil into a sauté pan, and heat over a medium flame. Place the mushrooms in the pan, without overcrowding, and brown them on one side, about 2 minutes. Turn them over and brown on the other side, another 2 minutes. Add salt to taste.

Cover the leeks with the mushrooms, sprinkle with the chopped chives, and serve.

José's tips

This is a great tapa when served on toasted bread. But it's also great as a side dish with any plain sautéed fish or chicken.

José's tips

Oyster mushrooms are perfect for this dish, but it works very well with any other wild mushrooms, or even with shiitake or small cremini mushrooms.

Hongos con patatas
Oven-roasted potatoes and oyster mushrooms

Serves 4

2 garlic cloves

1 tablespoon ham or bacon fat, diced

1/4 cup Spanish extra-virgin olive oil

1 medium Spanish onion, peeled and cut into strips (about 1 cup)

1/2 pound Idaho potatoes, peeled and cut into 1/4-inch-thick slices (about 2 large potatoes)

2 teaspoons salt

1 sprig fresh rosemary

2 tablespoons white wine

6 ounces oyster mushrooms (see tips), cleaned

1/2 cup Chicken Stock (page 222)

1/2 teaspoon chopped chives

Along the coast of Spain, it's very traditional to bake a whole fish with a layer of potatoes and onions underneath it. You can do the same with meats, too, roasting chicken or lamb on top of a layer of potatoes, onions, and green peppers—it makes for a wonderful meal. Here I'm applying the same technique, but using oyster mushrooms on top of the bed of potatoes and onions.

Heat the oven to 350 degrees.

Split the garlic cloves open by placing them on a chopping board and pressing down hard with the base of your hand or the flat side of a knife. Combine the fat, olive oil, and split garlic cloves in an ovenproof sauté pan over medium heat. Cook until the fat is rendered, about 2 minutes. Add the onions and cook until they are brown and soft, around 20 minutes. If the onions start to get too dark, add 1 tablespoon of water to cool things down and soften the onions. Add the potato slices, 1 teaspoon of the salt, and half the rosemary sprig. Toss together so the potatoes get coated in the oil.

Transfer the pan to the oven and bake for 20 minutes. Then remove it from the oven, add the wine, return it to the oven, and bake for 10 minutes to allow the alcohol to evaporate.

Remove the pan from the oven, and place the mushrooms on top of the potato-onion mixture. Add the chicken stock, and spoon some of the liquid from the bottom of the pan over the mushrooms. Return it to the oven and bake for another 15 minutes, basting as needed to make sure the potatoes and mushrooms don't dry out.

Remove the pan from the oven. Chop the remaining rosemary leaves and sprinkle them on top, along with the chives and the remaining teaspoon of salt. Serve immediately.

legumes

chapter 5

capitulo 5

Recipes

Garbanzos con espinacas
Moorish-style chickpea and spinach stew

Fabes con Almejas "Tia Chita"
Asturian bean stew with clams

Fabada asturiana
Traditional Asturian bean stew

Codorniz con lentejas
Quail with smoked bacon and lentil stew

Wine tips

Prima from the Toro region (Tinta de Toro grape)

Chivite "125 Aniversario" from the Navarra region (Chardonnay grape)

Paixar from the Bierzo region (Mencia grape)

Arrocal from the Ribera del Duero region (Tinta del Pais grape)

My home region of Asturias, in northern Spain, is a wonderfully undiscovered place. From the dramatic Costa Verde coastline to the towering Picos de Europa mountains, it's a region of small towns and villages where people live not so differently from the way they did a century ago. In the rustic village of Naves, where my uncle Gelín lives, they keep chickens, roosters, cows, and horses in their back-yards. They dry sheaves of corn, grow rows of vegetables, and store them in a *horreo*—an outbuilding that looks like a Japanese temple, raised on stilts to keep the food dry and safe from animals and bugs. Such buildings are almost sacred in Asturias, a reminder of how prized such dried foods are in Spanish culture.

None is more highly valued than *fabes,* the dried Asturian beans. In Naves you can still find elderly women who will sell you a bag of their special home-grown and home-dried *fabes.* Such beans are a world away from the dusty legumes you find in many supermarkets. Their thin skins are silky when dry and fabulously soft when cooked. In nearby towns such as Llanes, they even celebrate the *fabes* with a festival of traditional stews—restaurants serve multiple *fabadas,* showcasing the big, buttery white beans with chicken, chorizo, and lobster. Yet unlike stews elsewhere, it's not the meat or the fish that's the star; it's the bean, which breaks up in the cooking process, giving the stew a thick, creamy texture that is unforgettable.

Fabes are just one variety of legumes that feature prominently in Spanish food, especially home cooking. One of my fondest memo-ries of childhood is of returning home to the rich, warm smell of a garbanzo stew that my father was cooking. I would grab a plate and a spoon, climb onto a chair, and serve myself a big helping of gar-banzo and chorizo. That family pot of stew, and its dense aroma, is something I love to re-create here in my own home in Washington. It's the same for my wife, Tichi, who makes her family's garbanzo and spinach stew—a recipe she learned from her mother, who in turn learned it from her own mother. Tichi likes to serve it with an egg on top or on the side, and it's one of our daughters' favorite meals. (Coming from the south of Spain, Tichi's family cooking is heavily influenced by Moorish culture, and garbanzos are one of the best legacies of those centuries of Arab life.)

Often overlooked here, legumes are an intimate part of Spanish home life, one of the universal foods that unite rich and poor. They are also an easy, affordable, and delicious way to create true Spanish classics in any American home—especially as American supermarkets are now selling authentic Spanish beans, already cooked and conserved in glass jars. Most of the recipes here require day-before soaking, but the jars and cans of ready-to-use beans and chickpeas are a good shortcut if you don't have that much time.

José's tips

When the chickpeas are cooked and soft, you should have only around one finger's depth (¹/₂ inch) of water left in the bottom of the pan. If there is more, remove some water from the pan before adding the rest of the ingredients.

If you don't have time to cook for 2 or 3 hours, use 3 cups good-quality chickpeas from a can or jar. Just add some extra water before you cook the spinach, in case there isn't enough in the jar.

Garbanzos con espinacas
Moorish-style chickpea and spinach stew

Serves 4

9 ounces dried garbanzos (chickpeas)

1 pinch of baking soda

¼ cup Spanish extra-virgin olive oil

6 garlic cloves, peeled

2 ounces sliced white bread, crusts removed

2 tablespoons *pimentón* (Spanish sweet paprika)

1 pinch Spanish saffron threads

2 tablespoons Spanish sherry vinegar

½ pound spinach, washed

1 teaspoon ground cumin

Salt to taste

White pepper to taste

This was one of the first dishes my wife, Tichi, cooked for me, soon after we were married. It was also the cause for the most expensive telephone call we ever made, since she talked to her mother through the entire cooking process. The result was worth every penny. Now it's one of our Sunday specials—especially through the winter months.

The day before you plan to cook the stew, place the chickpeas in a bowl and cover with cold water. Add the baking soda, stir, and set aside to soak overnight. The next day, drain and rinse the chickpeas.

In a big saucepan, combine the chickpeas with 2½ quarts of water. Bring to a boil. Then reduce the heat to low and simmer until the chickpeas are tender, about 2 hours. Every 10 minutes or so, add ¼ cup of cold water to slow down the simmering. By the end, the water should have reduced so it is barely covering the chickpeas. Turn off the heat and let the chickpeas sit in the water.

Heat the olive oil in a small sauté pan over a medium-low flame. Add the garlic and cook until it is browned, about 3 minutes. Remove the garlic from the pan and set it aside. Add the bread to the pan and brown it on both sides, about 1 minute each side. Remove the bread and set it aside.

Remove the pan from the heat and allow it to cool for a few minutes. Add the *pimentón* and saffron to the pan, and then immediately add the sherry vinegar to prevent the *pimentón* from burning. Leave the pan off the heat.

In a mortar, smash the reserved garlic and the toasted bread to make a very thick paste.

Bring the chickpeas back to a low boil (see José's tips) and add the spinach. Simmer for 5 minutes. Add the *pimentón* mixture along with the garlic paste. You should have a thick, stewy sauce. Simmer for another 5 minutes. Season with salt and white pepper to taste, and serve immediately.

Fabes con Almejas "Tia Chita"
Asturian bean stew with clams

Serves 4

½ pound Asturian beans (see tips)

1½ quarts mineral or filtered water

1 Spanish onion, peeled

1 ripe plum tomato

¼ medium carrot, peeled

3 sprigs fresh parsley

4 tablespoons Spanish extra-virgin olive oil

Salt to taste

20 littleneck clams, cleaned thoroughly

Asturias, my home region, has some of the best beans you'll ever find—big and buttery, with thin skins—traditionally served with clams. The combination of the fresh texture of the clams with the creamy smoothness of the beans is just heavenly. It takes me right back to the Sunday lunches of my childhood with my Aunt Chita.

Place the beans in a bowl, cover with cold water, and set aside to soak overnight. The next day, drain and rinse the beans.

Combine the beans and the mineral water in a large stockpot and bring to a boil. Reduce the heat to low and simmer for 10 minutes, occasionally removing the foam on the surface. Then add the onion, tomato, carrot, and parsley, and simmer for 2 hours. Every 10 or 15 minutes, add ¼ cup of cold water to slow the simmering. Be sure the beans are always covered with liquid. By the end of the 2 hours, you should be left with 3 cups of water—enough to barely cover the beans.

Remove the vegetables and place them in a bowl or in a food processor. With a spoon, pick out ½ cup of beans that are split or broken. Add them to the vegetables along with 1 tablespoon of the cooking water. Blend together using a hand blender or food processor. Pass the mixture through a fine strainer, and return it to the beans in the stockpot. Add 2 tablespoons of the olive oil and season with salt. You should have very soft beans in a creamy, starchy broth. Bring to a simmer again. Bring 1 quart of water to a boil in a medium saucepan. Put 4 clams in the vigorously boiling water and cook until they open a fraction, just 5 seconds. Remove them from the water. Repeat with the remaining clams. With a paring knife, and holding the clams over a bowl, remove the clams from their shells, reserving the juices in the bowl. Set the clams aside. Strain the juices and add to the beans.

Place a ladleful of beans in the center of each soup dish, and arrange the clams on top. Drizzle the remaining 2 tablespoons of oil over the clams, and serve.

José's tips

If you can't find Asturian beans, or *fabes,* substitute another large dried white bean, like cannellini.

Pay attention when you place the clams in the boiling water. You're really just shocking them in the hot water for a few seconds, rather than cooking them. They'll continue cooking on top of the beans.

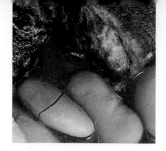

Fabada asturiana
Traditional Asturian bean stew

Serves 4

½ pound Asturian beans
(see tips)

1 quart Chicken Stock
(page 222)

2 chorizo sausages

2 blood sausages

¼ pound bacon, as a slab
(not sliced)

1 head garlic,
papery outer skin removed

1 onion, peeled

1 teaspoon *pimentón*
(Spanish sweet paprika)

1 pinch saffron threads,
crushed

½ cup Spanish
extra-virgin olive oil

José's tips

If you can't find *fabes,* which is the generic name for this big white bean from Asturias, you can substitute any other dried white bean that you can find in the supermarket. But the beans I'm talking about here are the best beans I've ever seen in my life. So it's worth the trouble to look for them at specialty stores or even to go online to find a supplier (see Sources, page 250).

When I visit my mother's family in my hometown of Mieres, there's nothing better at a big reunion than a huge bowl of *fabada.* This is not traditionally a tapa. Indeed, the way they serve it in Mieres, it's the opposite—it's a big, hearty plate, a dish from another era, when the menfolk worked long hours in the mines and the *fabada* was the perfect way to replenish at the end of the day. For me, it's also my favorite New Year's dish: the best comfort food. I wake up early and by 2:00 in the afternoon, we are ready to sit around the big stew. But you can also serve it as a tapa in a small cup. It's a wonderful taste of the region my family calls home.

The day before you plan to cook the stew, place the beans in a bowl and cover with cold water. Set aside to soak overnight. The next day, drain and rinse the beans.

Place the beans in a large pot and cover with the chicken stock. Add the chorizo, blood sausages, and bacon, along with the garlic and onion. Bring to a slow boil. At this point, you'll see white foam forming on the surface; remove it. Add the *pimentón,* saffron, and olive oil.

Continue to cook at a low simmer for 2½ hours. Every 10 minutes or so, add a little cold water to slow down the simmering. It's important to keep the beans covered with liquid so they cook properly. Remove the pot from the heat and allow the stew to rest for 1 hour.

Remove and discard the onion and garlic. Remove the bacon, blood sausages, and chorizo, and cut into thin slices.

The beans should have a thick and creamy consistency. If they're watery, take ½ cup of broken beans with a little stock, and crush them into a paste. Pass the paste through a sieve and return it to the stew to thicken it.

Fabada is traditionally served in the pot it was made in, with the meats served on a separate platter. Reheat the stew to a boil and serve it in bowls, with the slices of chorizo, sausage, and bacon on top.

José's tips
Try drizzling a little sherry vinegar on top of the lentils just before you serve them—it lifts the dish to another level. You can also experiment with other additions instead of quail, like squab or the classic chorizo.

Quail with smoked bacon and lentil stew

Serves 4

For the lentils

2 ounces smoked bacon
(about 1 thick strip),
cut into small cubes

1 tablespoon Spanish
extra-virgin olive oil

1 small onion, peeled and
finely chopped

1 small head garlic,
papery outer skin removed

1 carrot, peeled

1 small leek, well washed,
outer leaves removed

6 ounces dried lentils

1 quart Chicken Stock
(page 222) or water

1 bay leaf

1 sprig fresh thyme

½ teaspoon salt,
plus more to taste

For the quail

1 tablespoon Spanish
extra-virgin olive oil

2 whole quails,
boned and cut in half

Salt to taste

2 tablespoons sherry

Lentil stews are incredibly popular in Spain. They come on their own, or with chorizo and blood sausages. Or you can make them with a lighter meat, as we do here with quail. But a favorite of mine is a bowl of the lentils themselves, sprinkled with a little sherry vinegar just before eating.

Prepare the lentils: In a medium pot, sauté the bacon in the olive oil over medium heat until slightly brown, 2 to 3 minutes. Add the onions and cook until slightly translucent, about 3 minutes.

Add the garlic, carrot, leek, and the lentils. Pour in the chicken stock (or water) and bring to a boil. Reduce the heat to low and add the bay leaf and thyme. Simmer until the lentils are cooked, 20 to 30 minutes

Remove and discard the bay leaf and the thyme sprig. Pick out the garlic, carrot, and leek, and place them in a blender or food processor. Add 1 tablespoon of water and the ½ teaspoon salt, and blend to create a puree. Strain the mixture and set it aside. Leave the lentils in the pot, off the heat.

Cook the quail: Heat the olive oil in a small sauté pan over medium-high heat. Sear the quail pieces on the skin side until they are brown and crisp, about 3 minutes. Turn them over and cook for 1 more minute, but no more. You want the meat to remain juicy. Add salt to taste, remove from the pan and set aside.

Add the sherry to deglaze the sauté pan. Pour this into the lentils and mix together. Bring the lentils to a boil for 30 seconds to reheat.

Make a bed of lentils on each plate and place a piece of quail on top. Spoon a little of the garlic puree on the side, and serve.

peppers

chapter 6

capitulo 6

Recipes

Mejillones en escabeche
Cold mussel escabeche with vinegar and pimentón

Pimientos del piquillo confitados
Confit of piquillo peppers in their own juices

Pipirrana Andaluza con atún de almadraba
Tomato, green pepper, and cucumber salad with tuna in olive oil

Escalivada Catalana
Roasted eggplant, pepper, onion, and tomatoes, Catalan-style

Romesco
Catalan roasted-vegetable sauce

Guisantes tiernos al romesco
Spring green peas with romesco sauce and mint

Pimientos al ajo y vinagre de Jerez
Roasted red bell peppers with sherry vinegar

Wine tips

Viña Somoza from the Valdeorras region (Godello grape)

Barsao "Tres Picos" from the Campo de Borja region (Garnacha grape)

Gonzalez Byass "Amontillado del Duque" from the Jerez region (Palomino grape)

Gran Caus "Rosado" from the Penedes region (Cabernet Sauvignon grape)

Les Terrases from the Priorat region (Garnacha/Cabernet Sauvignon grapes)

Guelbenzu "Azul" from the Navarra region (Cabernet Sauvignon/Tempranillo grapes)

Bodegas Hidalgo-La Gitana "Palo Cortado Viejo Vos" from the Jerez region (Palomino grape)

pimientos

You could be forgiven for thinking it's a warehouse: a two-story concrete building located opposite an auto repair shop and next to a gas station. Inside there are conveyor belts and industrial-size vats. But the smell of soups and sauces tells another story. Felix Saenz is a traditional foodmaker in the Navarra region, producing jars of vegetables, meats, and seafood that Spanish cooks value highly. It may look like a small factory, but it's more like an oversize kitchen, where the work is done almost entirely by hand and the freshness of the ingredients is paramount. For twenty days at the end of September, Felix—like his competitors in nearby Lodosa—is consumed with a small, sweet, smoky red pepper, the piquillo. Piquillo peppers are a Spanish delicacy, roasted on a wood fire and painstakingly peeled by hand. They are conserved in their natural juices and olive oil, and sold in jars the world over—including the United States. They are justly famous for their intense sweetness and the quality of their preparation.

Piquillo peppers are also an insight into Spanish tastes. When they arrived from the New World, hot and mild peppers added a new element to European kitchens, already stocked with an extensive list of spices from the Far East. But the hot peppers that are so well known in America today failed to attain the same kind of popularity in Spain, where the European palate never liked really spicy food. Some of the milder peppers were simply transplanted, like the green bell peppers used in gazpacho or mixed with eggplant and tomatoes in *Pisto Manchego* stew. Other varieties took root in the Spanish soil and over many years emerged as new forms of peppers, only distantly related to their ancestors from South America. Typical of those is the piquillo. But there are also other famous varieties, like the *pimiento del padrón* from Galicia, which is a small, tasty green pepper that is almost always served fried, with a light sprinkling of salt. Some small farmers in California are beginning to grow these successfully now.

Perhaps the best-kept secret of Spain's pepper growers is that they produce the world's best *pimentón,* otherwise known as paprika. Hungary has become famous for its *pimentón* because it plays a starring role in the national dish, goulash. But Spanish *pimentón* is no less critical to some of our best-loved foods, such as the classic chorizo sausage and the *sobrasada,* a Majorcan pork sausage that mixes pork and *pimentón* into a creamy spread. It's also a vital ingredient for dishes such as *pulpo a la Gallega,* or Galician-style octopus. With a smokier flavor than its Hungarian counterpart, *pimentón* gives a rich, dense balance to the soft, fresh seafood we love so much all across Spain.

Mejillones en escabeche
Cold mussel escabeche with vinegar and pimentón

Serves 4

1 pound Prince Edward Island mussels, cleaned thoroughly

$1/2$ cup Spanish extra-virgin olive oil

3 garlic cloves

Zest of $1/4$ orange, removed with a peeler

$1/2$ tablespoon *pimentón* (Spanish sweet paprika)

$1/4$ cup sherry vinegar

$1/2$ teaspoon black peppercorns

1 sprig fresh rosemary

1 sprig fresh thyme

1 bay leaf

$1/4$ teaspoon salt

This tapa is one of those dishes that you'll find in most bars in Spain, made with canned mussels. But don't fool yourself. Sometimes those cans are very expensive, filled with the highest-quality mussels that have been perfectly cooked. Here we're re-creating a very popular tapa right at home, without opening an expensive Spanish can.

Bring 1 quart of water to a boil in a large pot. Place 10 mussels in a sieve and immerse it in the boiling water for 5 seconds, or just until the mussel shells open. Take the mussels out of the sieve and put them in a colander. Position a plate under the colander to catch the juices that will emerge from the mussels. Repeat until you have cooked all the mussels.

Take the mussels out of the colander, open them, and remove the flesh, being careful to keep them whole. Set them aside. Strain the water that has collected under the colander and place it in a small pan over medium heat. Cook until the mussel water is reduced to around $1/4$ cup, about 2 minutes. Set aside.

Heat the olive oil in a small sauté pan over medium heat. Split open the garlic cloves by placing them on a chopping board and pressing down hard with the base of your hand or with the flat side of a knife. Add the split garlic to the oil and brown it on all sides, about 2 minutes. Remove the pan from the heat and add the reduced mussel water, orange zest, *pimentón,* vinegar, pepper-corns, rosemary, thyme, bay leaf, and salt. Allow the escabeche to cool to room temperature; then pour it over the mussels. This dish usually tastes even better the day after you cook it.

José's tips

By scalding the mussels for a mere few seconds, you cook them just enough to be edible but not so much that they become chewy. This technique can be used for any bivalves.

Pimientos del piquillo confitados
Confit of piquillo peppers in their own juices

Makes 1 cup

25 piquillo peppers (Spanish wood-roasted sweet peppers), or one 13-ounce can

1 teaspoon sugar

2 garlic cloves, peeled

Salt to taste

1 cup Spanish extra-virgin olive oil

Piquillo peppers cooked this way are easy, fast, and unbelievably delicious. They can be enjoyed alone on a plate, on a slice of bread, or as a garnish with fish or meat. This is a traditional side dish in the steakhouses of northern Spain.

Heat the oven to 250 degrees.

Place 5 of the peppers in a small bowl, along with the sugar and 2 tablespoons of water. Use a hand blender to puree them well.

Arrange half of the remaining peppers in one layer in an 8-inch terra-cotta or ceramic casserole. (This works best when the peppers don't overlap.) Spoon half of the pepper puree on top, and smooth it out with the back of the spoon. Split open the garlic cloves by placing them on a chopping board and pressing down hard with the base of your hand or with the flat side of a knife. Scatter the garlic over the puree, and sprinkle with salt to taste. Make another layer of peppers, and cover with the remainder of the puree. Salt again.

Cover the peppers with the oil. Bake in the oven for 1½ hours, until they are completely tender. Remove, allow to cool to room temperature, and serve.

José's tips

To cook this dish successfully, you need more oil than you'll eat. Keep the leftover oil for dressings or for sautéing another dish later. The oil becomes infused with the pepper, and the taste is wonderful.

Pipirrana Andaluza con atún de almadraba
Tomato, green pepper, and cucumber salad with tuna in olive oil

Serves 4

For the tuna

3 cups Spanish extra-virgin olive oil

4 garlic cloves, peeled

1 tablespoon black peppercorns

1/2 pound top-quality fresh tuna

1/2 teaspoon sea salt

For the pipirrana

2 ripe plum tomatoes, prepared as 8 seed "fillets" and cubes of flesh (see page 40)

1/4 green bell pepper, seeded and cut into small cubes

1/2 cucumber, peeled and cut into small cubes

Sea salt to taste

2 tablespoons Spanish extra-virgin olive oil

1 tablespoon sherry vinegar

Pipirrana (sometimes known as *piriñaca*) is a different form of one of the most famous cold soups in the world: gazpacho. The traditional Andalucian soup is re-created here as a salad, using the same ingredients—a perfect example of how there can be two different approaches to the same traditional dish. *Pipirrana* goes well with many ingredients; here it's paired with fresh tuna that is poached in olive oil to maintain its freshness and moistness.

Prepare the tuna: In a medium saucepan, heat the olive oil to 160 degrees (measured with a candy thermometer). Add the garlic cloves and the peppercorns, and cook until the garlic is soft, about 7 minutes.

Remove the pan from the heat and allow the temperature to drop to 150 degrees. Season the tuna with the sea salt, and place it in the oil. It's important that the tuna be completely covered with oil so it cooks evenly. After 7 minutes, turn the tuna over and continue to poach for another 7 minutes. Keep the oil at a steady 150 degrees, returning the pan to the heat if necessary.

Remove the tuna and cut into the edge with a very sharp knife to check that it's done. The tuna should be a uniformly rosy color. (If it needs more cooking, return it to the oil, off the heat, and leave it until it reaches 110 degrees at its center, measured with a meat thermometer.) Set the tuna aside to cool; then slice it into eight 1/2-inch-thick cubes.

Prepare the *pipirrana:* Combine the cubes of tomato flesh with the green pepper and cucumber in a bowl, and season with sea salt. Add the olive oil and sherry vinegar and toss to mix.

To serve: Spoon the *pipirrana* onto a serving dish. Place the tuna pieces on top, then place the tomato-seed "fillets" around the tuna. Sprinkle with sea salt to taste and serve immediately.

José's tips

This is the same technique for preparing tomatoes that we used in the tomato salad (page 40). It's worth mastering, so you can really enjoy the tomato flesh at its best.

Escalivada Catalana
Roasted eggplant, pepper, onion, and tomatoes, Catalan-style

Serves 4

1 medium eggplant
(about ½ pound)

1 large Spanish onion

1 red bell pepper

3 large ripe tomatoes

¼ cup Spanish extra-virgin
olive oil, plus extra for
coating the vegetables

½ tablespoon
sherry vinegar

Salt to taste

White pepper to taste

Escalivada comes from the Catalan verb *escalivar,* which means to cook slowly, very close to the embers of a fire. The smokiness of the charcoal enriches the food and gives it an earthy quality. This recipe is for oven-roasting, but its soul comes from the open fire. It's a great dish on its own, but it's also perfect served alongside any grilled meat.

Heat the oven to 400 degrees.

Take all the vegetables, and using a brush, coat them with a thin film of olive oil. Place them in a baking dish or in a terra-cotta casserole, and roast in the oven for 40 minutes. Remove the eggplant, pepper, and tomatoes and set them aside. Leave the onion in the oven for another 20 minutes, until it too is soft. Remove and set aside.

The skins of the roasted vegetables will be soft and loose. When they are cool enough to handle, peel the vegetables. Seed the pepper and remove the top. Remove the top of the tomatoes and the eggplant with a knife.

Using your hands, tear the pepper into strips and each tomato into 3 or 4 pieces. Do the same to the eggplant. Using a knife, slice the onion into rings. Mix the vegetables together and place them in a serving dish. Cover them with the ¼ cup of olive oil and the sherry vinegar. Sprinkle with salt and white pepper, and serve.

José's tips
If you have a barbecue, the ideal way to roast the vegetables is on charcoal outdoors. In any case, this is a dish you can prepare days ahead and store in the refrigerator. It's wonderful served hot or cold.

Romesco
Catalan roasted-vegetable sauce

Makes 2 cups

½ cup Spanish extra-virgin olive oil, plus extra for coating the vegetables

1 red bell pepper

6 ripe plum tomatoes

1 head garlic, halved, papery outer skin removed

1 Spanish onion

3 ñora chili peppers (or any other dried sweet chili pepper)

¼ cup blanched almonds

1 ounce white bread, crust removed

1 tablespoon sherry vinegar

1 teaspoon *pimentón* (Spanish sweet paprika)

½ tablespoon salt

I have no doubt that this sauce will one day be found in every supermarket in America. It combines ingredients that everyone seems to love: peppers, tomatoes, almonds, bread, and onions. The original sauce comes from Tarragona, where people are to be proud of their own recipe. But the sauce wasn't always the main attraction; it started life as a fish stew, with different kinds of fish and shellfish. Today *romesco* is a cold sauce that is a wonderful match for vegetables, seafood, and meats.

Heat the oven to 350 degrees.

Brush a thin film of olive oil over the pepper, tomatoes, garlic, and onion. Place them in a medium roasting pan, and roast until all the vegetables are soft, 25 minutes.

While the vegetables are roasting, place the ñora chilies in a bowl and cover with hot water. Soak for 15 minutes. Strain, and remove the seeds. Place the chilies in a blender and puree until smooth. Pass the puree through a fine-mesh sieve into a bowl, and set aside.

Heat 1 tablespoon of the olive oil in a small sauté pan over low heat. Add the almonds and sauté to brown them a little, about 1 minute. Remove the almonds and set them aside.

Raise the heat to medium and add the bread to the pan. Cook until it becomes a nice brown color, around 30 seconds on each side. Remove the bread from the pan and set it aside.

Add the pureed ñora to the sauté pan and cook for 30 seconds. Remove from the heat.

Remove the roasting pan from the oven and set it aside. When the roasted vegetables are cool enough to handle, peel them. Seed the bell pepper and tomatoes, and cut off their tops. Place the roasted vegetables in a blender or food processor and add the almonds, toasted bread, pureed ñora, vinegar, *pimentón,* and the remaining 7 tablespoons of oil. Blend until it forms a thick sauce, and add the salt. Place the *romesco* sauce in a bowl.

José's tips

Here I add fresh bell pepper to the *romesco,* but traditionally we use only the dried ñora peppers that are so typical of Catalonian cooking. You can order a paste of ñora chili peppers through many websites that specialize in Spanish food (see Sources, page 250).

Guisantes tiernos al romesco
Spring green peas with romesco sauce and mint

Serves 4

2 tablespoons Spanish extra-virgin olive oil

½ cup chopped scallions

1½ cups shelled fresh green peas (from about 1½ pounds pea pods)

1 recipe Romesco (page 95)

16 small mint leaves

Salt to taste

Romesco is a very versatile sauce that can be used with a wide range of ingredients, from fish to vegetables and meats. I first ate this dish, prepared with baby fava beans, when I was seventeen years old. It was in a restaurant called Guria, in Barcelona, and I remember ordering three more plates because it was so good. I discovered this wonderful version with green peas at one of my favorite restaurants: San Pau, in San Pol, near Barcelona, where Carme Ruscadella—one of the finest chefs I've ever met—presides.

Heat the olive oil in a large sauté pan over a medium flame and cook the scallions for 5 minutes. Raise the heat to high, add the peas, and sauté for 1 minute. Remove from the heat.

Make a bed of *romesco* sauce on a serving plate. Place the peas and scallions on top of the *romesco,* and garnish with the mint leaves. Add salt to taste, and serve immediately.

José's tips
This technique is very versatile and can be the basis for several tapas. Instead of peas, you can make it with fava beans or even mushrooms.

Pimientos al ajo y vinagre de Jerez
Roasted red bell peppers with sherry vinegar

Makes 1½ cups

4 medium red bell peppers

½ cup Spanish extra-virgin olive oil

4 garlic cloves, peeled and thinly sliced

¼ cup mineral or filtered water

2 tablespoons sherry vinegar

Salt to taste

1 teaspoon chopped flat-leaf parsley

These are my mother's favorite peppers. The sweetness of the peppers and the acidity of the vinegar make for a perfect combination. The end result is a silky, shiny sauce—an emulsion of the gelatinous peppers, the olive oil, and the vinegar. It's wonderful on its own as a tapa, but it's also the perfect garnish for any meat, especially pork.

Heat the oven to 400 degrees.

Brush the peppers with a thin film of the olive oil and place them in a roasting pan. Roast for 30 minutes, turning them over every 10 minutes, until all sides are browned. Remove the pan from the oven and allow the peppers to cool. Then peel, seed, and tear them into strips. Set aside.

Heat the remaining oil in a medium saucepan over a medium flame. Add the garlic and cook until brown, about 1 minute. Add the peppers and mineral water, cover the pan, and cook on low heat, until the sauce has a silky texture and becomes emulsified, about 30 minutes. Add the vinegar, salt to taste, and the parsley. Serve immediately or allow to cool.

José's tips
You can serve this dish
hot or cold. It works well
on top of toasted bread,
or even as part of a salad.

vegetables
and more

chapter 7

capitulo 7

Recipes

Pisto Manchego con Flores de calabacín
Castilian-style zucchini and its flowers, with
peppers, eggplant, and tomato

Espárragos blancos de Navarra
White asparagus, Navarra-style

Espinacas a la Catalana
Spinach, Catalan-style

Judías verdes con tomate y cebolla
Green beans with tomatoes and pearl onions

**Guisantes tiernos y sus tallos a la menta fresca
con butifarra**
Sweet pea vines with sweet peas, mint, and
sausage

Alcachofas con jamón
Artichokes sautéed with ham

Wine tips

Higueruela from the Almansa region
(Garnacha grape)

Nekeas from the Navarra region (Chardonnay
grape)

Oliver Conti from the Emporda-Costa Brava
region (Sauvignon Blanc/Gewurstraminer grapes)

Mantel Blanco from the Rueda region
(Verdejo grape)

Fransola from the Penedes region (Sauvignon
Blanc grape)

Naia from the Rueda region (Verdejo grape)

verduras y más

I had always wanted to use zucchini flowers at my restaurants but could never find the right supplier at the right cost—until I visited a small Amish organic farm close by the Pennsylvania Turnpike eight years ago. There, among the heirloom tomatoes and sweet baby corn, I saw they were growing zucchinis in old tires. I spotted one plant that was in bloom, so I asked the young farmer, Daniel Beiler, if he would sell me the delicate flowers. I said I'd buy as many as he could grow, but he just scratched his long beard. He couldn't believe anyone ate them. A couple of months later, he called to say he was sending thirty cases of flowers to my restaurant. We created a lot of zucchini flower specials that month! Now Daniel is an expert grower of zucchini flowers, picking them just before they open so they last a little longer en route to the restaurant. He and his large young family have also learned to love eating them at home, coating them in eggs and flour and cooking them in butter. Daniel is proof that old and new traditions can come together in fresh ways that bring out the best in both.

Daniel is also part of a trend among smaller organic farmers who have introduced a city crowd to new fruits and vegetables. The best showcase for smaller farmers in my city is the market at Dupont Circle. Every Sunday for the last decade, more than two dozen organic producers have converged on a parking lot next to a bank in downtown Washington, D.C. In rain or in sweltering heat, they unload their trucks, set up some shelter, and lay out crates of the latest crops. Some sell the staple foods—corn, tomatoes, potatoes. But many others have brought new ingredients to a conservative town—sweet pea vines, Asian pears, Brandywine tomatoes. In a city where people work hard and shop at supermarkets, the Dupont Circle farmers' market has helped transform the way Washingtonians think about their fruit and vegetables, connecting city slickers to the fresh produce of the farmland around the nation's capital. The market is one of many around the country, part of a movement across America where small farmers have turned themselves into direct sellers, just as they did in the days before the big supermarkets. And just as they do in Spain today, where the farmers have gathered at marketplaces in small towns for centuries.

For me, the farmers' market has become a Sunday ritual. My daughters' baby food consisted of purees from those products— peas and carrots with a little chicken; potatoes, onions, and green beans. That led to several fights with my wife because whenever I fed my daughters, I took a little taste for myself. When my wife saw the empty bowl, I always told her the kids had eaten really well. She never believed me.

Pisto Manchego con flores de calabacín
Castilian-style zucchini and its flowers, with peppers, eggplant, and tomato

Serves 4

1 pound ripe plum tomatoes

6 tablespoons Spanish extra-virgin olive oil

2 garlic cloves

1/2 large Spanish onion, peeled and chopped into 1/2-inch cubes

1 sprig fresh thyme

1/2 small green bell pepper, seeded and chopped into 1/2-inch cubes

1/2 small red bell pepper, seeded and chopped into 1/2-inch cubes

1/3 medium zucchini, trimmed and chopped into 1/2-inch cubes

1/2 medium eggplant, trimmed and chopped into 1/2-inch cubes

4 zucchini flowers

Salt to taste

3 sprigs fresh parsley, finely chopped

Pisto Manchego is a classic dish: a perfect Mediterranean mix of vegetables—zucchini, peppers, eggplant, and tomato—and olive oil. This version is from La Mancha, the region at the heart of Spain. I've finished it off with zucchini flowers, which bring a wonderful seasonal freshness to the *pisto*.

Cut the tomatoes in half. Place a grater over a large mixing bowl, and rub the open face of the tomatoes into the grater until all the flesh is grated. Discard the skin. Strain the grated tomatoes and set aside.

Heat the olive oil in a medium sauté pan over a medium flame. Split open the garlic cloves by placing them on a chopping board and pressing down hard with the base of your hand or with the flat side of a knife. Add the garlic to the pan and sauté until it begins to brown, about 2 minutes. Add the onions and thyme, and sauté until the onions become translucent, about 5 minutes. Add the peppers and cook for 3 minutes, or until they start to soften. Add the zucchini and cook for another 3 minutes. The oil should be crackling lightly as the vegetables are cooking. Add the eggplant and cook for another 3 minutes.

Add the reserved tomato puree and cook until it turns a deep red color, 5 to 10 minutes.

Peel back the green base of the zucchini flowers and snap off the stems, pulling out the interior of the blossoms. Right at the end of the cooking time, add these blossoms to the *pisto* and remove the pan from the heat after just a few seconds. Season with salt to taste, sprinkle the parsley on top, and serve.

José's tips

If zucchini flowers are not in season, you can make this dish without them— it's actually more traditional without the flowers. I love eating *pisto* with a fried egg and a few slices of chorizo alongside.

José's tips

If you can't find white asparagus, you can sub-stitute green. Or you can use the great white asparagus, imported from Spain, that comes in a jar. Serve it, drained, straight from the jar with your specially cooked (and shelled) egg.

Espárragos blancos de Navarra
White asparagus, Navarra-style

Serves 4

8 large white asparagus, cleaned

Salt

1 large egg

2 tablespoons Spanish extra-virgin olive oil

Sea salt to taste

12 chive flowers, optional, for garnish

4 tarragon leaves, torn into pieces

This recipe uses a special technique for cooking eggs that leaves the inside runny but still thoroughly cooked. It's perfect for this springtime dish of white asparagus. As you cut through the egg, the asparagus become coated in the yolk, and the dish takes its shape and flavor before your eyes.

Cut off and discard the bottom 1 inch of each asparagus spear. Peel the remaining stalk, below the tip, with a sharp vegetable peeler to remove the bitter outer skin. Cut each spear into 2 pieces, 2 inches below the tip. Set aside the stalks and tops.

Prepare a bowl of ice water and stir in plenty of salt. Then fill a medium sauté pan with water and bring it to a boil. Add plenty of salt, lower the heat to a simmer, and cook the asparagus tops for 6 minutes. Remove the asparagus from the pan and immediately immerse them in the ice water.

Repeat with the asparagus stalks, boiling them for 20 minutes. Transfer the stalks to a blender and add a couple of tablespoons of the cooking water. Blend thoroughly; then strain and set the asparagus puree aside.

Fill a small saucepan with water and place it over low heat. Checking with a thermometer, heat the water to 147 degrees. Place the egg in the water, being careful not to break it, and cook for 35 minutes. Remove the egg from the water and set it aside.

Spoon the asparagus puree onto a serving plate. Carefully shell the flat end of the egg (not the more pointed top). Put the partially shelled egg on the puree and lift the rest of the shell from the top. Place the asparagus tops next to the egg. Drizzle with the olive oil, and season with sea salt to taste. Sprinkle with the chive flowers (if using) and the tarragon pieces, and serve.

Espinacas a la Catalana
Spinach, Catalan-style

Serves 4

2 tablespoons Spanish extra-virgin olive oil

1 golden delicious apple, peeled, cored, and cut into 1/4-inch cubes

1/4 cup pine nuts

1/4 cup seedless dark raisins

1/2 teaspoon salt, plus more to taste

10 ounces baby spinach, washed

Catalans love their dried fruits. One of the most popular desserts in Catalonia is the *postre de músico,* which is a glass of sweet wine, like a muscatel, served next to a little plate of almonds, pine nuts, and raisins—and any other dried fruit the musicians deserved. (That was the way the traveling troubadors got paid.) Here nuts and raisins are paired, not with a dessert wine, but with a vegetable. This is a super-fast dish, and you'll be eating like a musician in no time.

Heat the olive oil in a large pot over a high flame. When the oil is very hot, add the apple cubes and cook until they are a little browned, less than 1 minute. Add the pine nuts and cook until they are brown, about 20 seconds. Keep the pot moving so the nuts don't burn. Add the raisins and the 1/2 teaspoon salt, and stir together.

Add the spinach, mix, and sauté very fast until it starts to wilt. Then remove the pot from the heat; the spinach will continue to wilt off the heat. Add salt to taste, and serve immediately.

José's tips

This is a very quick dish to cook—so quick that you have to be careful not to burn anything. Be prepared beforehand, and be ready to serve it immediately. To make it extra-special, try preparing a quick pine nut praliné to serve with it: Toast additional pine nuts in a separate pan, then puree them with a little olive oil to make a very fine paste, like a smooth peanut butter. Drizzle the praliné over the plate and then top it with the spinach mixture.

Judías verdes con tomate y cebolla
Green beans with tomatoes and pearl onions

Serves 4

¾ pound green beans, trimmed

2 tablespoons Spanish extra-virgin olive oil

4 garlic cloves, peeled

4 pearl onions, peeled

4 cherry or baby tomatoes, halved

3 sprigs fresh thyme

Salt to taste

3 ounces *jamón serrano* (Spanish cured ham, see tips), torn into ribbons

Some American friends once told me they couldn't find vegetables in restaurants in Spain. But that doesn't mean that Spaniards don't eat them. The markets are full of fresh vegetables in season, and you always find great vegetable dishes in home cooking—they're just not necessarily on many restaurant menus. Every family has their own recipe for green beans, but this is one of my favorites. It's a simple, semi-cooked tapa that retains the freshness of the vegetables while mixing the flavors in the sauté pan.

Fill a medium pot with water and bring it to a boil. Fill a large bowl with ice water, and set it near the sink.

Add the green beans to the boiling water and cook until they are slightly al dente, 4 to 5 minutes. Drain the beans in a sieve, and immediately immerse them in the bowl of ice water. When they have cooled, drain and set aside.

Heat the olive oil in a sauté pan over medium heat. Add the garlic and cook for 2 minutes, or until slightly brown. Add the onions and sauté until they begin to brown slightly, 8 minutes. Add the tomatoes and cook until they start to become soft and release their juices, 1 minute. Add the blanched green beans and the thyme, and cook for another 2 minutes, or until the beans are cooked through.

Season with salt to taste, mix in the pieces of ham, and serve immediately.

José's tips

Look for *jamón serrano*, Spanish cured ham, to finish this dish. If you can't find it, you can substitute bacon, or even cubes of pork to create a really hearty dish. Add the bacon or pork at the beginning of the process, when you sauté the garlic.

Guisantes tiernos y sus tallos a la menta fresca con butifarra

Sweet pea vines with sweet peas, mint, and sausage

Serves 4

3 tablespoons Spanish extra-virgin olive oil

1/2 cup finely chopped white onion (about 1/2 large onion)

1 medium leek, well washed, outer leaves removed, finely chopped

2 ounces bacon (about 1 thick strip), cut into small cubes

1 *butifarra* or pork sausage (see tips), removed from the casing and crumbled

1 tablespoon all-purpose flour

2 tablespoons anise-flavored liqueur, such as anisette

1/2 cup Chicken Stock (page 222) or water

1 sprig fresh mint plus 12 small leaves, washed

1 1/2 cups shelled fresh green peas (from about 1 1/2 pounds pea pods)

1/4 pound sweet pea vines

Salt to taste

This is a classic dish for the late spring, when you can find fresh peas and pea vines at your local farmers' market. It's amazing to see how the pea vines taste so much like the peas themselves. This dish is perfect for a family meal. My kids love to shell the peas as we prepare the dish together, and they love eating the end result even more.

Heat the olive oil in a medium saucepan over a medium-low flame. Add the onions and the leeks, and cook, stirring occasionally, until the onions are soft and slightly browned, 10 to 15 minutes. Add 1 tablespoon of water to soften the onions further. The water will spit until it evaporates, leaving the onions thoroughly cooked without getting burned. Add the bacon and sausage, and cook gently until the sausage has browned, about 4 minutes.

Stir in the flour and the liqueur, and cook for 30 seconds. Pour in the chicken stock (or water) and raise the heat to medium. Add the mint sprig and bring to a boil. Then lower the heat to a simmer, add the peas and the vines, and cook for 5 minutes, or until tender. Season with salt to taste.

Spoon a little on each plate, sprinkle the mint leaves on top, and serve immediately.

If fresh peas aren't available, you can get a close approximation by using good-quality frozen peas that are sweet and tender.

If you can't find a good Spanish *butifarra* sausage, any good-quality, sweet pork sausage will do. But you can also skip the bacon and pork sausage—it will still be a wonderful dish.

José's tips

One day supermarkets here will sell fresh artichoke hearts that are already cleaned, as in Europe today. Until then, although cleaning an artichoke may seem difficult, it's worth the trouble. When it comes to keeping the hearts white, use parsley, as I do here, instead of the traditional lemon. Lemon makes the artichokes too acidic; the parsley enhances the white color of the flesh.

Alcachofas con jamón
Artichokes sautéed with ham

Serves 4

4 large or 6 baby artichokes

1 bunch flat-leaf parsley, with 1 teaspoon chopped parsley reserved

3 tablespoons Spanish extra-virgin olive oil, plus extra for drizzling

1½ cups juice from canned tomatoes

1 pinch sugar

¼ teaspoon salt, plus more to taste

2 tablespoons dry white wine

1 ounce *jamón serrano* (Spanish cured ham), diced (about 2 thin slices)

1 bay leaf

Despite their look, artichokes are not a difficult vegetable to cook. Here they're paired with ham (almost any vegetable—asparagus or green beans, for instance—marries well with ham, because of its natural saltiness).

Using a serrated knife, cut off and discard the top half of each artichoke. Using your fingers, remove and discard the first few layers of leaves, until you reach the tender leaves beneath. Use a spoon to remove and discard the white, hairy interior. Use a paring knife to remove and discard the tough outer layer around the base of the artichoke, until you reach the soft white flesh. Peel the stalk until you reach the white flesh again. Don't be afraid to remove most of the artichoke. Repeat with all the artichokes.

Cut the trimmed artichokes into 6 or 8 segments, and put them in a bowl of cold water. Add the bunch of parsley (to stop the artichoke from oxidizing and coloring).

Heat 1 tablespoon of the oil in a small pan over a medium flame. Add the tomato juice and sugar. Simmer for 15 minutes, until the juice is a deep red.

Heat the remaining 2 tablespoons of oil in a sauté pan over a medium flame. Add the artichokes, making sure they lie flat, and the salt. Sauté, stirring every 30 seconds, until the artichokes are golden, 2 to 3 minutes. Add the wine and simmer until reduced by half, about 30 seconds. Add the ham and stir for 10 seconds; pour in the reserved tomato juice. Add the bay leaf and cook until the artichokes are tender, 3 to 4 minutes. Add salt to taste. Drizzle with a little more oil, sprinkle with chopped parsley, and serve.

citrus

chapter 8
capitulo 8

Recipes

Escarola con sanguina, queso de cabra, almendras
y vinagreta de ajo tostado
Frisée with blood oranges, goat cheese, almonds,
and garlic dressing

Bogavante con clementinas, pomelo y limón
al azafrán
Lobster with clementines and grapefruit,
in saffron oil

Ensalada de naranjas con granadas
Valencia orange and pomegranate salad with
olive oil and sherry vinegar

Naranjas al vino tinto
Oranges in red wine

Mermelada de naranja con yogur
Orange marmalade with yogurt and frozen
orange

Wine tips

Jose Pariente from the Rueda region
(Verdejo grape)

Pazo de Señorans from the
Rias Baixas region (Alvariño grape)

Viña Mein from the Ribeiro region
(Treixadura grape)

Pesquera Crianza from the Ribera del Duero
region (Tinta del Pais grape)

Casta Diva "Cosecha Miel" from the Alicante
region (Moscatel grape)

cítricos

Each fall, something fascinating happens at supermarkets across the United States: Small wooden boxes pile up by the hundreds, carrying a tiny label that reads "Product of Spain." Inside are dozens of ripe, juicy clementines. It may seem naïve to be proud of something like this, but this is a Spanish product that truly has made its mark in America in the last few years. Although other countries have tried, nobody else has achieved the quality, the sweetness, and the seedlessness of the Spanish clementine. Part of the Chinese mandarin family, clementines found their real home in the soil and climate of Spain in the last century. Now it seems that everyone loves them. They are easy to peel, and their membranes are whisper-thin. Best of all, they are incredibly juicy, with a great balance of acidity and sweetness that makes them irresistible. Seeing them here brings back memories of the days when we used to buy fruit from Rosa la Frutera at her store in Santa Coloma de Cervelló. My mother would buy ten pounds of clementines, which my three brothers and I would demolish in two days. We'd eat them like peanuts.

Such indulgence seems very modern to many older people in Spain. Whenever the fruit bowl was passed around my family table, my mother Marisa used to remind us children that there were many homes where they couldn't afford fruit. It may seem hard to believe now, when we have such a wide variety of fruit available, but for many years after the Second World War, fruit was nothing less than a luxury.

Citrus fruits are often pigeonholed as an ingredient for desserts, but in fact they are tremendously versatile. With its range of flavors, citrus is one of the most fascinating food groups. In the same orange you can taste sweetness, acidity, and bitterness. If you add a little salt, you have all the elements that make up our sense of taste. Whether it's the clementine or high-quality Valencia oranges, Spain's citrus fruits can be the centerpieces of salads, seafood dishes, and, of course, desserts.

José's tips

You can use endive instead of frisée, placing the orange, cheese, and almonds inside each endive leaf. It's great as finger food, with the endive functioning as a boat that holds the rest of the salad.

Blood oranges have a limited season; if you can't find them in your area, clementines are a good substitute.

Escarola con sanguina, queso de cabra, almendras y vinagreta de ajo tostado

Frisée with blood oranges, goat cheese, almonds, and garlic dressing

Serves 4

For the dressing

2 tablespoons fresh orange juice

1 tablespoon plus ½ cup Spanish extra-virgin olive oil

1 garlic clove, peeled

2 teaspoons sherry vinegar

1 teaspoon sea salt

For the salad

15 blanched almonds, cut into small pieces

3 blood oranges (see tips)

1 medium head frisée lettuce (see tips), washed, leaves separated (about ¼ pound)

¼ pound fresh goat cheese, crumbled into small pieces

The first time my mother-in-law, Pilar, came to our house, she didn't much like anything I cooked. Then one day I found out that her favorite food was almonds. All of a sudden, when I added almonds to the food, things she wouldn't eat before became fantastic dishes. I started to add almonds to all my meals, and that's how this salad came about. Now she likes my cooking a little more.

Prepare the dressing: Put the orange juice in a small sauté pan and cook over a medium flame until reduced by half, about 1 minute. Set aside.

Heat 1 tablespoon of the olive oil in a small sauté pan over a very low flame, and sauté the garlic clove until it is soft, about 3 minutes (do not let it brown).

Place the garlic in a blender, along with the remaining ½ cup olive oil, the sherry vinegar, and the reduced orange juice. Mix until thoroughly blended. Add the sea salt. Set the dressing aside.

Make the salad: Place a small sauté pan over medium-low heat. Add the almonds, and toast, stirring regularly to ensure they don't burn, 3 to 4 minutes, or until they turn light brown. Set them aside.

Slice off the tops and bottoms of the oranges. Using a paring knife, cut off all the peel and pith by cutting around the oranges. Slice along the sides of each segment and pull out the segments.

Place the frisée in a serving bowl, and top it with the orange segments, the cheese, and the toasted almonds. Add the dressing, toss, and serve.

Bogavante con clementinas, pomelo y limón al azafrán
Lobster with clementines and grapefruit, in saffron oil

Serves 4

½ cup salt,
plus more to taste

1 lobster
(about 1¼ pounds)

¼ cup Spanish
extra-virgin olive oil

1 pinch saffron threads

½ cup fresh orange juice
(from about 1 large orange)

2 clementines, peeled

Grated zest of 1 lemon

1 orange

½ pink grapefruit

Sea salt to taste

Where I grew up, lobsters were so expensive that they were treated like royal treasure. If you got four or five pieces of lobster meat in a restaurant, it would be a big deal. But when I came to America, I discovered Maine lobsters—one of the best bargains in the world.

Bring 3 quarts of water to a boil in a large pot. Add ½ cup of salt. Submerge the lobster in the water, cover, and boil for 6 minutes. Remove the lobster and set it aside to cool. Working over a bowl to catch the juices, cut the tail from the body and remove the tail shell. Set aside the shelled tail meat.

Working over the same bowl, remove the shell from the claws with a nutcracker or mallet. Remove the meat, discarding the fatty part at the tip of the claws. Pull off and discard the legs, and pull apart the head. Using a spoon, transfer the gray meat from inside the head to a small bowl. Using a hand blender, puree the reserved juices and gray meat until smooth. Combine the puree with the meat from the claws.

Heat the oil in a small pan over a low flame. Add the saffron and warm gently for 20 seconds. Remove from the heat and set aside for 6 minutes, allowing the saffron to infuse the oil. In a small saucepan, heat the orange juice over a medium flame until reduced by half; set aside. Separate the clementines into segments and cut off the membranes. You'll end up with hundreds of tiny bits of pulp. In a mixing bowl, whisk together the clementine pulp, saffron-infused oil, reduced orange juice, lemon zest, and salt to taste.

Slice off the top and bottom of the orange. Cut off all the peel and pith by cutting around the orange. Slice along the sides of each segment, and pull out the segments. Repeat with the grapefruit. Set aside.

To finish the lobster, slice the tail meat into 4 medallions and sprinkle with a little sea salt.

To serve, place the claw meat on a plate, and arrange the orange and grapefruit segments on top. Top with the lobster medallions. Pour the dressing over the salad, and serve.

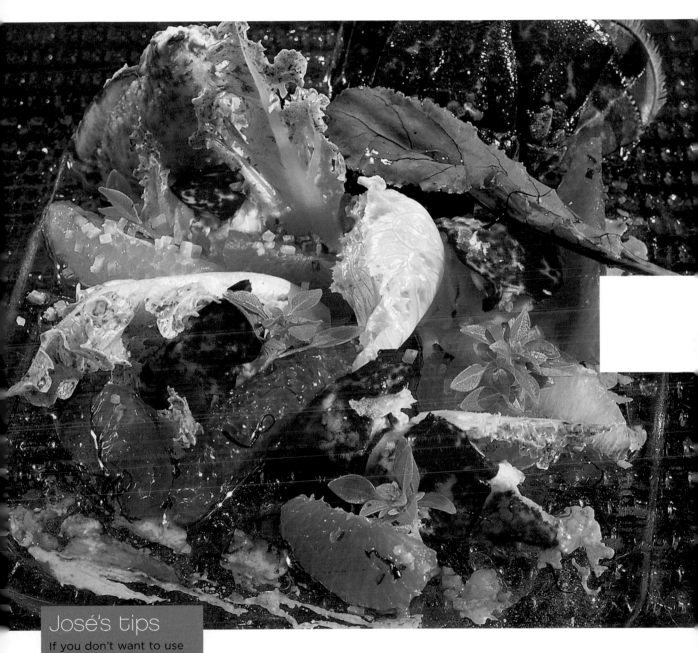

José's tips

If you don't want to use lobster, try stone crab claws or Chesapeake lobster.

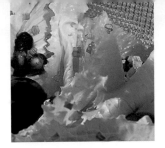

Ensalada de naranjas con granadas
Valencia orange and pomegranate salad with olive oil and sherry vinegar

Serves 4

1 pomegranate

4 Valencia oranges

½ cup Spanish extra-virgin olive oil

1 garlic clove, peeled

2 teaspoons sherry vinegar

Salt to taste

1 head romaine lettuce, washed and torn into pieces

¼ cup black olives, pitted

1 tablespoon chopped chives

The season for oranges and pomegranates overlaps for some time into the fall, making these two fruits a natural match. Both have a unique sweetness and tartness that is complemented by the olives' saltiness. This is a fresh salad that's wonderful for a late-summer lunch.

Slice the pomegranate in half. Turn one half face-down above a large bowl, and hit the back of it with a large spoon. The fleshy seeds will fall into the bowl. Repeat with the other half. Remove the white pith and set the seeds aside.

Slice off the tops and bottoms of the oranges. Rest them on a chopping board and, using a chef's knife, cut off all the peel and pith by cutting around the oranges. Slice along the sides of each segment, and pull out the segments. Set aside.

In a small skillet, heat 1 tablespoon of the olive oil over a very low flame. Add the garlic and sauté until soft, about 3 minutes (do not let it brown). Place the garlic in a blender, add the remaining 7 tablespoons of olive oil and the sherry vinegar, and mix until thoroughly blended. Add salt to taste.

In a serving bowl, mix the lettuce with the reserved orange segments and pomegranate seeds. Add the olives and the dressing, and toss. Sprinkle with the chives, and serve.

José's tips
You can add walnuts for extra crunch, or even some toasted croutons to make it more of a main dish.

Naranjas al vino tinto
Oranges in red wine

Serves 4

For the syrup

2 cups good Spanish red wine, such as Navarra or Ribera del Duero

Zest of 1 lemon, removed with a peeler

Zest of 1 orange, removed with a peeler

2 cloves

1 teaspoon juniper berries

1 cinnamon stick

$^3/_4$ cup sugar

3 star anise pods

For the fruit

4 Valencia oranges

1 lemon

6 small mint leaves

Orange flowers (or any edible flowers), optional, for garnish

When I was sixteen, I visited Lausanne, Switzerland, on a school trip. At that age I had both soccer heroes and chef heroes. Fredy Girardet was one of my chef heroes, next to Ferran Adrià and Pierre Gagnaire. With not much money in my pocket, I got on a bus with two friends and went to see his restaurant in the tiny town of Crissier. I still remember the thrill of simply being close to the restaurant. As we looked around the building and sneaked a peek at the menu, the chefs spotted us and invited us into the kitchen. We probably spent four hours there. It was one of the most amazing experiences I'd ever had. In the shop next to the restaurant I bought Girardet's cookbook, and over the next few weeks I cooked the whole book. One of my favorite recipes in it is a great dessert of apples in red wine—the inspiration for this dish. (By the way, I had to decide between buying the book and paying for the bus fare back to Lausanne. I chose to hitchhike.)

Prepare the syrup: In a medium saucepan, combine the wine, lemon and orange zest, cloves, juniper berries, cinnamon stick, sugar, and star anise. Bring to a boil, then reduce the heat to low and simmer until the mixture is reduced by one third, about 25 minutes. Strain the mixture and refrigerate until it is thoroughly cooled. Then check the syrup's consistency: it should be like honey. If it's too thin, return it to the pan and reduce for a few more minutes. If it's too thick, add a little water until you achieve the proper consistency.

Prepare the fruit: Slice off the tops and bottoms of the oranges. Rest them on a chopping board and, using a chef's knife, cut off all the peel and pith by cutting around the oranges. Slice along the sides of each segment, and pull out the segments. Set aside. Repeat with the lemon.

Spoon the syrup onto a plate and arrange the orange and lemon segments over it. Sprinkle the mint leaves and orange flowers (if using) on top, and serve.

José's tips
This can also be served
with vanilla ice cream or
a sponge cake for a full
dessert.

Mermelada de naranja con yogur
Orange marmalade with yogurt and frozen orange

Serves 4

5 Valencia oranges

³⁄₄ cup plus
9 tablespoons sugar

¹⁄₂ cup heavy cream

7 ounces (1 cup minus
1 tablespoon) good-quality
plain yogurt

2 cups fresh orange juice

When I was growing up, I ate yogurt every day. Usually the yogurt was plain, and we added some sugar or honey to make it sweeter. One day we ran out of both sugar and honey. All we had was orange marmalade, so we tried that instead. It was great! This dish is inspired by those days.

Juice 3 of the oranges and strain the liquid. Place the strained juice in the freezer and leave it until frozen through, 1 hour.

Make the marmalade: Place the remaining 2 oranges in a pot of cold water to cover. Bring it to a boil, remove from the heat, and drain. Refill the pot with fresh water and repeat three times, using clean water each time. This blanching process removes the bitterness from the orange peel. Cut the blanched oranges—peel and all—into ¹⁄₄-inch cubes, and place them in a medium pot with ³⁄₄ cup of the sugar. Cook over low heat for 1 hour, stirring occasionally, until the oranges are very soft and have mixed with the sugar to form a marmalade. Set it aside.

Whip the heavy cream in a chilled bowl until light and fluffy. In another bowl, whisk the yogurt and 2 tablespoons of the sugar together. Slowly fold one fourth of the whipped cream into the yogurt. Repeat with another fourth of the cream, folding slowly as you go. Repeat again, until you've incorporated all the cream. Chill this mousse in the refrigerator until cold, about 30 minutes.

Combine the 2 cups orange juice and the remaining 7 tablespoons sugar in a saucepan over low heat. Simmer until it has reduced to a thick sauce, 10 minutes. Set it aside.

Remove the frozen juice from the freezer. Using a small spoon, scrape out small pieces of the frozen juice.

To serve, place 2 tablespoons of the marmalade on each plate. Drizzle a bit of the sauce (the orange reduction) around the plate. Spoon the mousse on top of the marmalade, creating a mound that is about ¹⁄₂ cup in size. Scoop out a small hole at the top of the mousse and fill it with frozen juice pieces. Serve immediately.

José's tips

This dessert might sound complicated, but you can make most of it well in advance: the orange juice can be frozen the day before you need it, and the marmalade can be made earlier in the week.

garlic and onions

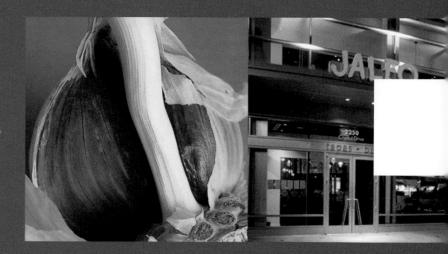

chapter 9
capitulo 9

Recipes

Sopa de ajo
Castilian garlic soup

Calamares a la plancha con ajo y perejil
Squid with garlic and parsley

Pollo al ajillo
Chicken with garlic

Gambas al ajillo
Traditional garlic shrimp

Ajo blanco Malagueño
Almond, garlic, and grapes gazpacho

Coca de cebolla con pimientos, anchoas y queso
Manchego
Traditional Catalan flatbread with caramelized
onions, roasted peppers, anchovies, and Manchego
cheese

Cebollas al Cabrales
Roasted Vidalia onions with Cabrales cheese

Calçots al estilo de Valls
Early spring onions with romesco sauce

Calamares encebollados
Squid with caramelized onions

Revuelto de ajetes
Creamy eggs with shallots and scallions

Wine tips

Elias Mora from the Toro region
(Tinta de Toro)

San Vicente from the Rioja region
(Tempranillo grape)

Pujanza from the Rioja region
(Tempranillo grape)

Grambazan "Ambar" from the Rias Baixas
region (Alvariño grape)

Fino "Tiopepe" from the Jerez region
(Palomino grape)

Ayles Tinto "Joven" from the Cariñena region
(Garnacha/Cabernet Sauvignon/Merlot/
Tempranillo grapes)

Cervoles from the Costers del Segre region
(Chardonnay grape)

Finca Dofi from the Priorat region
(Garnacha/Cabernet Sauvignon grapes)

Abadia de Cova from the Ribeira Sacra
region (Godello grape)

Remelluri Blanco from the Rioja region
(Moscatel/Viognier/Rousanne grapes)

ajo

In Cervantes's classic book, Don Quixote admonishes his squire, Sancho Panza, about one of the oldest and most popular features of the Spanish diet: "Eat neither garlic nor onions for thy smell will betray the peasant in thee." He wasn't the only one to have strong feelings about the popularity of garlic. Three centuries earlier, in 1330, King Alfonso of Castile issued a decree forbidding any knights who ate garlic or onion from appearing in court, or from speaking to other courtiers, for four weeks. Garlic has long been described as the spice of the lower classes in Spain, but like so many humble ingredients, it is central to Spanish cooking. There's nothing more Spanish than a piece of toasted bread rubbed with a raw garlic clove and sprinkled with a little salt and olive oil. In fact, olive oil, garlic, and bread are the staples of the Man of la Mancha. They are also the elements—along with a little water—of *sopa de ajo,* one of the most humble and delicious soups anywhere in the world. In fact, garlic may well be the only ingredient that is shared across all of Spain's regions and all of Spain's kitchens. It's more varied than you might think: While garlic is known for its strong flavor, it can also be exceptionally delicate, as is the case with the very best *ajo morado,* or purple garlic, that comes from Banyoles in Girona to the north, and from Las Pedroñeras in Cuenca in the heart of Spain.

Americans are fascinated by garlic as much as Spaniards are. At Jaleo, my tapas restaurant in Washington, D.C., the garlic dishes are some of our best sellers—tapas like *gambas al ajillo,* where the garlic adds depth and warmth to the shrimp. This classic tapa gave me my biggest break as a cook: I was just a teenager, working my first summer as a chef in a small seafood restaurant called L'Antull in the fishing town of Rosas. One late summer night, a young chef from a nearby restaurant stopped for a quick bite. That chef was Ferran Adrià, and a few months later I was working in his kitchen. His restaurant, El Bulli (created with his partner Juli Soler and Ferran's brother Alberto), would become the most original restaurant of the last decade. Ferran became my mentor, my inspiration, and my very good friend—and all thanks to some fresh shrimp and a few cloves of garlic.

cebollas

One of the best examples of marrying American ingredients with Spanish tapas is the Vidalia onion from Georgia, which I often mix with my mother's favorite cheese, Cabrales, from my home region of Asturias. Vidalias are unbelievably light and sweet—sweeter than our everyday Spanish onions, so sweet you could almost eat them like an apple. They are the perfect balance for the deep, sharp flavor of the Cabrales. Cheese and onion are not normally mixed like this in the traditional tapas you find in Spain. Yet the ingredients are, on their own, typically Spanish. By using what I call association—matching two ingredients that may never have been married before—you can create recipes that are both contemporary and authentic.

Not all onions are like Vidalias, but that doesn't mean they can't become soft and sweet in your kitchen. A term you'll see here frequently is "caramelization." What does that mean? It's a process where the heat transforms the onion's acids into sugars, and the sugars then caramelize. It's really two processes, or chemical reactions, that take place only if you give them enough time. What you end up with is an onion that has a unique aroma, a deep brown color, a sweet flavor, and a soft texture. At his superb restaurant, Mugaritz, near San Sebastián, my friend Andoni Luis Aduriz slow-roasts onions in clay to give them a wonderfully earthy aroma. Here we use the simpler method of slow-cooking in a sauté pan, with the help of a little water and a lot of patience. If you're well organized and you know that a recipe calls for caramelization, you can cook the onions a day or two beforehand and store them in the refrigerator. When you master this technique, you'll see that it takes the same time to cook one onion as it does ten onions. You can use the caramelized onions to take your sauces and stews to another level, or you can simply add them to a burger for an amazing topping.

Sopa de ajo
Castilian garlic soup

Serves 4

3 tablespoons Spanish
extra-virgin olive oil

6 garlic cloves,
peeled and sliced

2 tablespoons white wine

½ tablespoon *pimentón*
(Spanish sweet paprika)

3 ounces rustic white bread,
crust removed, torn into
small pieces

1 quart Chicken Stock
(page 222)

2 large eggs, beaten

Salt to taste

1 tablespoon chopped
flat-leaf parsley

Wherever I go in my travels, I find Spanish people who are proud that they know how to make this traditional Castilian dish, no matter which region they come from. My good friend Magín Revillo, the Washington correspondent for Radio Nacional de España (Spanish National Radio), makes one of the finest garlic soups I ever tasted—even though he grew up in Barcelona.

Heat the olive oil in a medium saucepan over a medium flame. Add the garlic and sauté until golden brown, about 1 minute. Add the wine and cook until the alcohol evaporates, about 30 seconds. Then add the *pimentón* and sauté for 1 minute.

Add the bread and pour in the chicken stock. Stir together and bring to a boil. Once it reaches a boil, reduce the heat to low and simmer for 8 minutes.

Add the eggs and stir with a spatula to fold them into the soup. The eggs will form long strands, almost like noodles. Simmer for 2 more minutes, and add salt to taste. Sprinkle with the parsley and serve.

José's tips

You can make this soup with water if you like. That's the traditional way, but I find that chicken stock makes it richer and tastier. Instead of adding the beaten eggs, you can poach 1 whole egg per person: just break the eggs into the barely simmering soup and leave them for 2 or 3 minutes without disturbing.

Calamares a la plancha con ajo y perejil
Squid with garlic and parsley

Serves 4

3 tablespoons Spanish extra-virgin olive oil

4 small squids, tentacles separated, washed and dried

1 garlic clove, peeled and finely chopped

Juice of ¼ lemon (about ½ tablespoon)

½ tablespoon finely chopped flat-leaf parsley

Salt to taste

This dish represents the essential simplicity of Spanish cooking: a high heat, a little oil, and some fresh ingredients. It is traditionally cooked on a flat griddle—*la plancha*—which is one of the most popular cooking techniques in Spain. The *plancha* is a small version of the griddles you see in American diners, where they're used for pancakes or burgers. Every Spanish home has a *plancha* for cooking seafood, but you can also use a good-quality frying pan.

In a flat griddle or a medium frying pan, heat 1½ tablespoons of olive oil over a medium-high flame. Place the bodies of the squid in the pan and sear them, without moving them, for 3 minutes. Turn them over, add the tentacles, and cook for 1 minute. Then turn the tentacles over and cook for 1 more minute. Remove the squid from the pan, and place it on a serving dish.

Add the remaining 1½ tablespoons oil and the garlic to the pan, and sauté for 20 seconds. Remove from the heat.

Sprinkle the lemon juice over the garlic and stir together. Sprinkle the parsley into the mixture, pour it over the squid, and add salt to taste. Serve immediately.

José's tips
You can try this recipe with any other shellfish, such as mussels, clams, or shrimp.

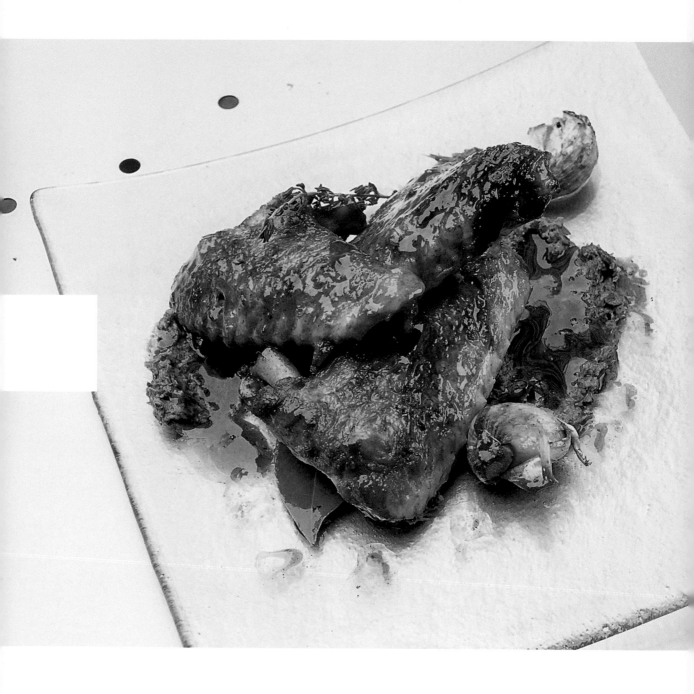

Pollo al ajillo
Chicken with garlic

Serves 4

10 garlic cloves

¼ cup Spanish extra-virgin olive oil

12 chicken wings (see tips), cut in half at the joint

3 sprigs fresh thyme

1 bay leaf

¼ cup Spanish Manzanilla sherry

¼ cup Chicken Stock (page 222)

Salt to taste

Black pepper to taste

Chicken may seem fairly ordinary, but until recently it was an expensive item in Spain. Not so long ago, this dish was a combination of a poor man's ingredient (garlic) with a rich man's ingredient (chicken). It's now a classic tapa. The sauce you're left with—an emulsified mixture of the olive oil, the natural juices of the chicken, and the sherry—is perfect for dipping bread.

Split open the garlic cloves by placing them on a chopping board and pressing down hard with the base of your hand or with the flat side of a knife. Heat the olive oil in a large sauté pan over a medium flame, add the garlic, and sauté until it is lightly browned, 3 to 4 minutes.

Add the chicken wings and sauté until browned on all sides, 5 minutes. Add the thyme, bay leaf, and sherry. Stir the mixture well so the oil and sherry emulsify, and simmer for 1 minute. Add the chicken stock and cook for 1 more minute. Add salt and pepper to taste, and serve.

José's tips
You can use chicken legs, cut into small pieces, if you don't want to use the wings. And if you like mushrooms, sauté some wild mushrooms with the chicken, or even use dried chanterelles, to add another dimension to this classic.

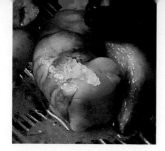

Gambas al ajillo
Traditional garlic shrimp

Serves 4

¼ cup Spanish
extra-virgin olive oil

6 garlic cloves,
peeled and thinly sliced

20 large shrimp
(about 1 pound),
peeled and deveined

1 guindilla chili pepper
(or your favorite dried
chili pepper)

1 teaspoon brandy

1 teaspoon chopped
parsley

Salt to taste

This is the ultimate tapa—no other dish is simpler, faster, or more rewarding to your taste buds. There's no better way to set the mood for an evening of tapas. Just be sure to include some good bread to soak up the delicious sauce.

Heat the olive oil in a medium sauté pan over a medium-high flame. Add the garlic and sauté until browned, about 2 minutes.

Add the shrimp and the chili pepper. Cook for 2 minutes. Turn the shrimp over and sauté for another 2 minutes. Pour in the brandy and cook for another minute. Sprinkle with the parsley, add salt to taste, and serve.

José's tips

This tapa depends on great shrimp. You can use previously frozen shrimp, if that's all that is available. But if you're able to find fresh shrimp from North Carolina or the Gulf of Mexico, or even the small red Maine shrimp that are available for a short time around January, you'll make a dish you'll never forget.

Ajo blanco Malagueño
Almond, garlic, and grapes gazpacho

Serves 4

7 ounces blanched almonds (see tips)

1 garlic clove, peeled

3 cups mineral or filtered water

3 ounces white bread, torn into small pieces

½ cup Spanish extra-virgin olive oil, plus more for drizzling

2 tablespoons sherry vinegar

1 teaspoon salt

16 seedless grapes, peeled

Ajo blanco is the grandfather of the red gazpacho, the tomato-based cold soup that has won such international renown. Its simple ingredients speak volumes about its origins: the combination of water, bread, and garlic was one of the first meals to feed poor people working the fields under the sun of southern Spain. Later, the Moors brought almonds, which added extra nutrition and flavor to the soup. It would take the discovery of the New World's tomatoes to create the famous red gazpacho; *ajo blanco* is how it all started.

Combine 1 cup of water, the almonds, and the garlic in a medium pot and bring to a boil. When the water reaches a boil, drain.

Pour a fresh cup of water into the pot, and add the drained almonds and garlic; bring to a boil. Drain once again. By now the garlic will have lost much of its strength and the almonds will be softened.

Place the garlic and almonds in a blender. Add the mineral water, bread, ½ cup olive oil, vinegar, and 1 teaspoon salt. Blend until smooth.

Place a colander over a large bowl, and line it with cheesecloth. Pour the soup into the colander. Once most of the liquid has passed through the colander, gather the cheesecloth around the remaining solids and squeeze gently to release as much liquid as possible from the solids. Discard the solids. Pour the soup into a pitcher, and chill it for at least 30 minutes.

To serve, place 4 grapes in each shallow soup bowl. Drizzle a little circle of olive oil around the edge of each bowl. Pour the *ajo blanco* into the bowls at the table.

José's tips
Look for Spanish Marcona almonds—many supermarkets sell them already roasted. They are a wonderful garnish. Other great garnishes include lobster pieces or sautéed wild mushrooms.

José's tips

If you don't want to make the dough, there are a couple of options. You can buy ready-made bread dough from your local bakery (if you ask them, they should sell it to you). Or you can buy puff pastry dough and roll it very thin. Remember to make lots of holes with your fork to ensure that the dough doesn't rise too much.

Coca de cebolla con pimientos, anchoas y queso Manchego

Traditional Catalan flatbread with caramelized onions, roasted peppers, anchovies, and Manchego cheese

Serves 4

For the onions

¼ cup Spanish extra-virgin olive oil

1 Vidalia onion, thinly sliced

For the flatbread

½ ounce (2 envelopes) active dry yeast

½ cup whole milk, at room temperature

1 cup plus 3 tablespoons all-purpose flour, plus extra for work surface

½ teaspoon salt

20 black olives, pitted and cut into small pieces

One 13-ounce jar piquillo peppers (Spanish wood-roasted sweet peppers), cut into ½-inch-wide strips

16 anchovy fillets (oil-packed)

6 ounces Manchego cheese, grated (about 1 cup)

Spanish extra-virgin olive oil, for drizzling

Sea salt to taste

2 tablespoons chopped chives

Bread with a roasted topping seems to be a registered trademark of the Italian kitchen. But this is also a very traditional and popular way of cooking in Catalonia. Instead of pizza, we have *coca*—hundreds of varieties of sweet and savory *cocas*. What distinguishes *cocas* from their Italian cousins is the almost complete absence of cheese and tomato. This version uses Spanish ingredients that are easily found in supermarkets across the United States.

Prepare the onions: Heat the olive oil in a medium saucepan over medium-low heat. Add the onions and cook, stirring occasionally, until soft and brown (caramelized), around 30 minutes. If the onions start to get too dark, add ½ tablespoon of water to keep them cooking evenly without burning. Set them aside.

Make the flatbread: In a small bowl, stir the yeast into the milk. Place the flour and salt in a food processor, add the yeast mixture, and process for 60 seconds, until you have a well-mixed dough. Cover the bowl with plastic wrap and set it aside at room temperature for 30 minutes to allow the dough to rise.

Meanwhile, heat the oven to 350 degrees.

Take out the dough and knead it for 5 minutes. Then cut the dough into 8 equal pieces and roll each piece into a ball. Sprinkle a little flour on your work surface and roll a ball of dough out to form a very thin long strip, around 10 inches long and 2 inches wide. Prick the strip with a fork. Repeat seven more times, creating 8 strips of dough.

Cover the strips of dough with the caramelized onions and the olives. Place on a baking sheet and bake until crisp, 10 minutes. Remove the baking sheet from the oven, leaving it on.

Cover the *cocas* with a layer of piquillo pepper strips. Add 2 anchovies on top of each, and sprinkle with the grated cheese. Return to the oven for 2 minutes.

Drizzle the *cocas* with olive oil, add sea salt to taste, and sprinkle with the chopped chives. Serve hot.

Cebollas al Cabrales
Roasted Vidalia onions with Cabrales cheese

Serves 4

3½ tablespoons Spanish extra-virgin olive oil

½ teaspoon cider vinegar

1 large egg yolk

1 pinch of salt, plus more to taste

2 Vidalia onions, unpeeled, each cut into four ½-inch-thick slices

2 ounces baby green lettuce leaves

2 ounces Cabrales cheese (see tips)

1 tablespoon pine nuts

1 teaspoon chopped chives

The first time I tasted a sweet Vidalia onion, I developed this dish on the spot, in my head. It has since become one of the most popular tapas at Jaleo. The sweetness of the onion balances the sharpness of the cheese, which is cut by the cider vinaigrette.

Heat the oven to 350 degrees.

Prepare the dressing: In a mixing bowl, whisk together 2 tablespoons of the olive oil and the vinegar. Add the egg yolk and pinch of salt, and mix thoroughly to create a thick vinaigrette. Set it aside.

In a small roasting dish, use your hands to rub the remaining 1½ tablespoons of oil all over the onions. Place the dish in the oven and roast for 30 minutes; the onions should be soft and brown. Remove the pan from the oven, allow the onions to cool, and then remove the outer skin.

Toss the lettuce in the dressing. Place a few lettuce leaves on each plate, arrange some onions on top, and add salt to taste. Crumble the cheese over the onions, and sprinkle with the pine nuts and chives. Drizzle with a little of the dressing that remains in the bowl, and serve.

José's tips
If you can't find Cabrales, use another good blue cheese, like Stilton or Gorgonzola.

Calçots al estilo de Valls
Early spring onions with romesco sauce

Serves 4

28 spring onions
or thick scallions

1 recipe Romesco
(page 95)

Calçots, or spring onions, normally take over a year to grow, in a long process that produces a thicker, sweeter onion than the more familiar scallion. You can find something similar in Asian markets across the United States. One very special Spanish tradition, which I think has a great future in America, is the *calçotada.* As winter draws to an end in February, we look for *calçots,* or early spring onions. We grill them on a wood fire, then wrap them in newspaper, where they steam off the grill. When we take them out of the paper, we smash off the bottoms and pull out the perfectly cooked hearts. We dip the hearts into *romesco* sauce, and eat their soft sweet half by lowering them carefully into the mouth. I can still remember seeing the food critic Gael Green devouring them at a *calçotada* organized by my friend Rosendo at his farmhouse near Barcelona. It was an honor to be part of a family reunion and to taste one of the sweetest rites of the end of winter.

Prepare a very hot charcoal grill.

Place the spring onions directly on the grill rack and cook until the outer edges are slightly burned, 6 to 8 minutes. Remove them from the grill and wrap them in newspaper. Place them in a warm place close to the fire for 15 minutes.

When you are ready to serve the onions, open the newspaper and transfer the onions to individual plates. To eat them, smash the bottom of each onion and remove the heart from the burned outer skin by pulling it up from the top. Dip the white base in the *romesco* sauce, and place it directly in your mouth.

José's tips

This has to be done on a grill in order to capture the heat and the natural smokiness of the charcoal. Wrapping the grilled onions in newspaper and keeping them close to the fire allows them to keep cooking. The result is a deliciously soft heart that is easy to pull out of its burned outer layers.

Calamares encebollados
Squid with caramelized onions

Serves 4

¼ cup Spanish extra-virgin olive oil

1 garlic clove, unpeeled

1 Spanish or Vidalia onion, thinly sliced

1 bay leaf

Salt to taste

¾ pound fresh squid (see tips), cleaned and cut into small triangles

2 tablespoons dry white wine

1 teaspoon chopped flat-leaf parsley

As a young chef working on the Spanish coast during the summer, one of my very favorite meals was the one we would prepare after a long night of partying. We would go to the beach at 6:00 a.m. to greet the fishermen as they arrived in their small boats. Those fishermen caught their squid one by one, using an old technique that allowed them to trap the squid without the squid releasing its precious ink. With a pound or two of fresh squid in our hands, we would return to the kitchen, light up the *plancha* (griddle), and sear the squid while they were still alive, without cleaning them. Today this is still one of my all-time favorite breakfasts.

Heat the olive oil in a large sauté pan over a medium flame. Split open the garlic clove by placing it on a chopping board and pressing down hard with the base of your hand or with the flat side of a knife. Add the garlic to the pan and cook until it starts to brown, about 2 minutes.

Add the onions and bay leaf, and cook slowly until the onions are light brown, about 10 minutes. Then reduce the heat to low and cook, stirring occasionally, until the onions are soft and tender (caramelized), about 20 minutes. If the onions start to get too dark, add ½ tablespoon of water. Remove them from the pan with a slotted spoon and set aside, leaving the oil in the pan.

Raise the heat to high and sprinkle a little salt on the oil. Add some of the squid, making sure you don't overcrowd the pan—you need to leave plenty of space between them so the heat remains high and the squid is sautéed, not boiled. Sauté for 15 to 20 seconds on each side. Remove the squid from the pan and repeat the process with the remaining squid.

Return all the squid to the pan, add the caramelized onions, and stir together. Pour in the wine and boil for around 20 seconds. Sprinkle with the parsley, and serve.

José's tips

If the squid are really fresh, which you can find occasionally, they don't need to be cleaned. You'll know they're fresh when they have a nice brilliant finish and a slightly gray color. The outer skin turns pinkish when the squid is no longer fresh.

Creamy eggs with shallots and scallions

Serves 4

2 teaspoons Spanish
extra-virgin olive oil

4 shallots, peeled and sliced

8 scallions, peeled,
cleaned, and thinly sliced
on the diagonal

½ small green bell pepper,
seeded and finely chopped
(about ¼ cup)

4 large eggs

2 tablespoons heavy cream

Salt to taste

White pepper to taste

1 tablespoon chopped chives

4 slices white bread,
toasted

This is a very traditional dish that is served in bars for breakfast, or as a sandwich with tomato toast (see page 36). The best I ever had was at Pinotxo, a twelve-seat bar at the entrance to the Boquería market, where Juanito greets Barcelonians and tourists alike with his amazing charm. Make sure you stop at Pinotxo's and ask for one of his special milky coffees to go with your eggs and onions. It's spectacular.

Heat the olive oil in a large sauté pan over a medium-high flame. Add the shallots and sauté until soft and almost translucent, 1 minute. Add the scallions and cook for 1 minute. Add the green pepper and cook for another 3 minutes.

Break the eggs into a bowl, add the cream, and whisk for 3 seconds. Pour the eggs into the scallion mixture in the hot sauté pan, and remove it from the heat.

Scramble the eggs, stirring them slowly with a wooden spoon. The eggs are done when they are a creamy, runny mixture. Season with salt and white pepper to taste, sprinkle with the chives, and serve with toast to mop up the plate.

José's tips

This dish is better when the eggs are not over-cooked—scrambled eggs should be soft and runny. With the pan on a medium-high heat, it is ready very quickly.

rice

chapter 10

capitulo 10

arroz

When I was a young boy, I used to help my father, Mariano, cook the best-known dish in Spanish cuisine: paella. We had this huge paella pan, almost a meter in diameter, that could feed more than a hundred people. Because we didn't have a big home, my father loved to invite dozens of friends to the countryside in the spring and summer for a spectacular paella. He would put me in charge of the open fire. I would add more wood when my father needed it at the beginning of the paella process, just after adding the rice. Then, when the heat reached its peak, I would help move the charcoal away from under the paella pan to ensure that the rice wouldn't overcook. Without knowing any better, I thought that my father had relegated me to the most menial, sweaty, and simple job around the paella pan. It was only many years later that I realized that he had actually given me the single most important task in creating paella.

Just like the classic American barbecue, it's all about the fire. Paella began life as a country meal, using the ingredients of the surrounding fields and the heat from burning vines. Like the barbecue, paella cooking has traditionally been the preserve of the menfolk, cooking for large groups of friends in the open air. And even though we don't use firewood in today's kitchens, controlling the heat is still the most important task of anyone aspiring to cook classic paella. The paella is not strictly the food itself, but the large, flat round pan we use to cook the rice (just as the barbecue isn't the meat, but the grill it sits on). This two-handled pan is the perfect medium for the heat; as the liquid reduces, the oil and proteins inside the paella mixture seal in the heat, cooking the rice underneath. That's why it's so important to resist the temptation to dip your finger or a spoon into the rice while it's cooking. If you break the film on the surface, the heat will escape as if from a chimney and the rice will cook unevenly. Paella pans range from small (for two people) to huge (for five hundred people). For the recipes here, a twelve-inch paella pan is ideal; you can find one at one of the websites listed in the Sources section. (You can also use a large sauté pan.)

Of course, rice is the key ingredient in any paella, and it's good to get to know the different varieties we have in Spain. When we talk about rice, we are mainly talking about short-grain rice like Bomba from Valencia, which looks like a little ball, or Calasparra from Murcia, which is a little longer in shape. These are becoming increasingly available across the United States. But if you can't find either, you can substitute Arborio. (Never use a long-grain or parboiled rice.) That's true of the other rice dishes in this chapter as well. Just remember that different varieties of rice cook in slightly different ways. If you use a rice that isn't Spanish, you'll need to check on the side of the box for the right quantity of stock or water to use.

People often expect rice to be a side dish to other ingredients: chicken, seafood, fresh vegetables. Yet the real star of these recipes is the rice and nothing but the rice.

Paella de pollo y setas
Chicken and mushroom paella

Serves 4

2 tablespoons Spanish
extra-virgin olive oil

2 chicken legs,
cut into small pieces

1/2 pound fresh mushrooms,
such as chanterelles

3 ounces green beans, cut into
1-inch pieces

1/2 garlic clove, peeled and finely
chopped (about 1 teaspoon)

2 tablespoons chopped *jamón
serrano* (Spanish cured ham)

1/4 cup dry white wine

1/4 cup Sofrito (page 37)

1 quart Chicken Stock
(page 222)

1 pinch saffron threads

1 bay leaf

1 tablespoon salt

1 1/2 cups Spanish Bomba or
Calasparra rice, or Arborio rice

José's tips

In this paella you can add
some extra vegetables,
such as eggplant, zuc-
chini, cauliflower, or any
of your favorites. Just
sauté the vegetable with
the mushrooms, after the
chicken. You can also add
chicken livers with the
mushrooms for extra fla-
vor, or substitute rabbit
for the chicken.

I can remember as a child listening to the older generation talking about the days when chicken was served only on special occasions in the little towns across Spain. People had few chickens and little grain to feed them, so they'd wait for a birthday or a festival to kill the birds and make a spectacular stew. This is an homage to those days, when chickens were something special and the dishes that featured them were the center-piece of a feast.

Heat the olive oil in a paella pan over high heat. Add the chicken and sauté until it is very brown on all sides, about 8 minutes. Remove and set aside.

Add the mushrooms to the paella pan and sauté until they are golden, about 3 minutes. Add the green beans and the garlic, and cook for 3 minutes. Return the chicken to the pan, along with the ham.

Pour in the white wine and cook until it is reduced by half, about 1 minute. Add the *sofrito* and cook for 3 minutes. Pour in the chicken stock and bring to a boil. Crush the saffron and add it to the pan, along with the bay leaf. Season with the salt. (Make sure it's just a little salty, because when you add the rice, the dish will balance itself out.)

Add the rice, taking care to spread it evenly around the pan. Cook for 5 minutes on a high flame, stirring frequently with a wooden spoon. You'll see the rice floating around the pan. If it's not, add an extra 1/2 cup of stock or water.

Reduce the heat to low and cook at a slow boil for 10 minutes, or until the liquid is absorbed. Never put your finger or a spoon into the paella during this cooking, or the rice will cook unevenly.

Remove the pan from the heat and let it sit for 3 minutes. The stock should be absorbed by the rice and there should be a nice shine to the top of the paella. Serve immediately.

Arroz con leche como hacen en Mieres
Rice and milk, Mieres-style

Serves 4

10 cups whole milk

1 strip lemon zest

1 cinnamon stick

1 cup Spanish Bomba or Calasparra rice, or Arborio rice

4 tablespoons unsalted butter

1 cup sugar

Arroz con leche is the dessert that best reflects Asturian cooking. Mieres is my hometown, and I return there as often as I can to visit my family. Asturias doesn't produce rice, but it's undoubtedly one of the best milk-producing regions in Europe, with its green pastures and mountains. In Washington, I buy a local organic milk from Blue Highland Dairy that reminds me a lot of Asturian milk—full of cream and flavor—for this wonderfully creamy dish.

Combine the milk, lemon zest, and cinnamon stick in a large pot and bring to a boil. Once the mixture boils, remove the cinnamon stick and the lemon zest.

Stir in the rice, reduce the heat to low, and simmer for 30 minutes. Keep stirring with a wooden spoon to make sure the rice does not stick to the bottom of the pot.

Add the butter and simmer for another 5 minutes. Add the sugar and mix vigorously. Remove the pot from the heat and spread the rice on a platter. Leave it to rest. As it cools, the milk will develop a thin skin on the top of the rice; fold this into the rice before serving. The pudding will be ready when it reaches room temperature, in 3 or 4 hours. You can also serve it cold from the refrigerator the next day.

José's tips

If you want a richer rice, add 3 egg yolks after removing the pot from the heat. You can also sprinkle some sugar on top and caramelize it with a torch. When you take the rice off the heat, the mixture should not be too compact, because it will become even denser as it cools down. You can always add some extra hot milk later if it becomes too dense.

Paella de bogavante a banda
Lobster paella

Serves 4

1 small Maine lobster
(1 to 1¼ pounds)

2 tablespoons Spanish
extra-virgin olive oil

6 ounces fresh squid,
cut into small pieces

¼ cup Sofrito (page 37)

1 garlic clove, finely chopped
(about 1 teaspoon)

3½ cups Traditional Fish
Stock (page 184)

1 pinch Spanish
saffron threads

1 tablespoon salt

1½ cups Spanish Bomba
or Calasparra rice (see tips)

Bogavante, or clawed lobster, should not be confused with the clawless spiny lobster called *langosta,* which has a more delicate and subtle flavor. In Spain both are considered a delicacy and are available only at a very high price, mainly because they are wild and hard to catch. When I first came to New York and visited the Fulton Fish Market, in downtown Manhattan, I couldn't believe my eyes: the *bogavante* lobsters cost less than $4 a pound! This paella is the perfect showcase for the lobster, proving that the best paellas are those with just one or two main ingredients.

Using a very sharp knife, separate the lobster head from the tail. Cut the lobster head in half, putting the blade between the eyes. Slice through the head cleanly, then cut it into quarters, and cut the claws in half. Cut the tail into 6 medallions.

In a paella pan over high heat, sear the lobster medallions in the olive oil for 1 minute. Remove them from the pan and set them aside. Add the squid to the pan and sear for 15 seconds. Add the *sofrito,* stir, and cook for 1 minute. Add the garlic, reduce the heat to low, and cook for 3 minutes.

Pour in the fish stock, raise the heat, and bring to a boil. Crush the saffron and add it to the pan. Season with the salt. (Make sure it's just a little bit salty; the rice will balance out the saltiness.)

Add the rice, taking care not to dump it in a pile—spread it evenly around the pan. Cook for 5 minutes over high heat, stirring frequently with a wooden spoon. You'll see the rice floating around the pan at this stage. If it's not, the mixture is too dry and you should add another ½ cup of stock or water.

Place the lobster head, claws, and medallions on top and reduce the heat to low. After this point, never put your finger or anything else in the rice. If you do, you will break the natural film that forms on top of the paella and the rice will cook unevenly. Maintaining a slow boil, cook for 10 minutes, or until all the liquid is absorbed.

Set the paella aside for 3 minutes; then serve right away.

José's tips

If you can't find Bomba or Calasparra, Arborio rice is the next best thing. Just be careful to check the box for the perfect quantity of stock. Each rice is slightly different and you'll need to use your judgment.

Arroz con almejas
Traditional rice with clams

Serves 4

2 cups Traditional Fish Stock (page 184)

4 tablespoons Spanish extra-virgin olive oil

1/2 Spanish onion, peeled and very finely chopped

1 garlic clove, peeled and very finely chopped

1/4 carrot, cut into small cubes (about 1/2 cup)

1/2 cup Spanish Bomba or Calasparra rice, or Arborio rice

1/3 cup dry white wine

Salt to taste

12 Manila or other small clams

5 asparagus spears, cut into small pieces

2 tablespoons finely chopped parsley

José's tips

It's always nice to add a touch of raw olive oil on top when you serve this dish. I love to make it without cooking the clams, serving them raw out of the shell. I simply put the raw clams on top of the cooked rice—the heat of the rice is enough to steam the delicate clams. You can make the same dish with mussels instead of clams.

If there's something Americans and Spaniards share, it's a passion for clams—and for eating them raw. (What we don't do so often in Spain is to fry them, which my friend Bob Kinkead does with Ipswich clams at his restaurant in Washington, D.C.) This simple rice dish maintains the best of the unique, fresh clam flavor. It's not raw, and it's certainly not fried—it's a delicious something in between.

Bring the fish stock to a boil in a saucepan. Once it reaches a boil, reduce the heat to low and maintain a simmer.

Combine 3 tablespoons of the olive oil, the onions, and the garlic in a large sauté pan over medium heat. Cook slowly for 5 minutes, being very careful that the onions do not turn brown—you want them to be soft and translucent.

Add the carrots to the sauté pan and cook for another 5 minutes. Add the rice and cook for 2 minutes. Add the wine and cook until reduced by half, about 30 seconds. Pour in 1 1/2 cups of the hot fish stock and a little salt to taste. (Take care with the salt because the clams add their own saltiness to the rice.) Cook over medium heat, stirring occasionally, until the rice is silky and creamy, 14 minutes.

In a separate small pan, bring the remaining 1/2 cup of fish stock to a boil. Once it begins to boil, add the clams and the asparagus. Cover, and cook until all the clams are open; depending on their size, this will take 1 to 2 minutes.

Add the clam mixture, the parsley, and the remaining tablespoon of olive oil to the rice and stir well. Bring to a boil. Once it reaches a boil, remove from the heat and serve immediately.

Arroz negro con calamares y gambas
Black rice with squid and shrimp

Serves 4

3 squid (about
6 ounces total), cleaned

Salt to taste

1 quart Traditional Fish
Stock (page 184)

2 garlic cloves, peeled
and finely chopped

2 tablespoons chopped
flat-leaf parsley leaves

4 tablespoons Spanish
extra-virgin olive oil

2 tablespoons Sofrito
(page 37)

1 cup Spanish Bomba
or Calasparra rice, or
Arborio rice

4 teaspoons squid ink
(see tips)

8 medium shrimp, shelled
and deveined

Spanish fishermen have a technique for catching squid with a hook so the squid cannot use its defense mechanism of squirting ink to protect itself. The squid caught this way—*calamares de potera*—have their ink sacs intact and are highly prized; they cost three or four times more than squid caught in a normal net. Black rice with squid, or even more traditionally with cuttlefish, is a dish I love to cook at home. Of all the rice dishes we have in Spain, this is one of the most distinctive.

You can serve this with Allioli (pages 20 and 22) on the side or mixed in with the rice.

Slice the squid along the sides to open them up. Cut the heads into small pieces, and cut the bodies into small triangles. Sprinkle with a little salt.

Bring the fish stock to a boil in a medium saucepan. Once it reaches a boil, reduce the heat to low and maintain a simmer. Make sure the stock is a little salty for your taste, because when you add the rice, the seasoning will balance out.

Combine the garlic, parsley leaves, and 2 tablespoons of the olive oil in a cup. Blend to create a smooth paste (or smash them together with a mortar and pestle).

Pour the remaining 2 tablespoons of oil into a terra-cotta (or metal) casserole over a medium flame. Place the squid in the oil and sauté, stirring with a spoon, until slightly brown, 1 minute. Stir in the *sofrito* and cook for 1 minute. Stir in the rice and cook, stirring frequently, for 1 minute. Add the squid ink, and stir in the hot fish stock. Stir in the garlic mixture and maintain at a medium simmer for 5 minutes.

Add the shrimp and simmer for another 10 minutes. Serve hot.

José's tips

If you can find cuttlefish, use it instead of the squid. Cuttlefish has a very distinctive flavor, and traditionally black rice is made with it.

If the squid or cuttlefish are fresh, look for a tiny black bag inside the body. Smash this sac with a fork and mix the ink with the stock. This is the natural ink, and it will make your rice taste like the sea.

cheese
and eggs

chapter 11

Recipes

Solomillo al Cabrales
Slow-roasted beef tenderloin with Cabrales cheese

Ensalada de manzanas con Murcia al vino
Apple and Murcia cheese salad with walnuts

Queso Idiazábal marinado al romero
Marinated Idiazábal cheese with rosemary

Queso Manchego con pan con tomate
Manchego cheese with Catalan tomato bread

"Mel i Matò"
Cheese and honey

Huevos fritos con chorizo y patatas
Fried eggs with Spanish chorizo and potatoes

Revuelto de espárragos trigueros
Scrambled eggs with tender asparagus

Flan al estilo de mi madre
Spanish flan in my mother's style

Huevos de codorniz con huevas de trucha
Quail eggs with trout roe

Tortilla de atún de almadrava
Tuna omelet with a twist

Wine tips

Artadi "Viña el Pison" from the Rioja region
(Tempranillo grape)

Roda I from the Rioja region (Tempranillo grape)

Casa La Ermita from the Jumilla region
(Syrac/Monastrel grapes)

Muga Reserva from the Rioja region
(Tempranillo grape)

La Orbe from the Rioja region (Tempranillo grape)

El Vinculo from La Mancha region
(Tempranillo grape)

Fuente Elvira from the Rueda region
(Verdejo grape)

Ochoa Dulce from the Navarra region
(Moscatel grape)

Agustin Torello "Kripta" Brut Natural Gran
Reserva from the Cava region
(Xarello/Macabeo/Parellada grapes)

Gonzalez Byass Palo Cortado "Don Chivarita"
from the Jerez region (Palomino grape)

High up in the mountains of Asturias, where the clouds drift over the salmon-spawning waters of the Cares River, the rocks hide a network of damp limestone caves. For centuries, the shepherds of the region would spend the spring and summer on the high pastures nearby, turning the milk from their sheep into cheese for the rest of the year. The limestone caves were the perfect place to store their precious supplies and the ideal environment in which to create a rich blue cheese like Cabrales. Today the Cabrales caves hold trays upon trays of pungent, yellowing rounds of cheese. After the cheeses have dried on wood shelves for twenty days and aged in the caves for four months, penicillin spores spread through the cheeses' natural holes, and the resulting blue mold is spectacular. Nowadays Cabrales may be made with a mixture of cow's and sheep's milk, but the sharp, creamy taste is just the same. When I first came to New York and was feeling homesick, I walked into Dean & Deluca and saw a piece of Cabrales. I bought a little bread, spread the Cabrales on top, and felt comforted as I watched Manhattan go by.

From a smoky Idiazábal to the red-wine-infused Murcia al vino, Spanish cheeses are as varied as they are exquisite. In Asturias, the blue cheeses range from the powerful Cabrales to the creamy, delicate Gamonedo. In the plains of La Mancha, they make the classic Manchego—perhaps Spain's best-known cheese. Such variety helps to make Spanish cheese an exceptionally versatile part of our cuisine.

These glorious products of Spain's regions are no longer so hard to find in the United States. In Williamsburg, Virginia, there's a small company run by Tim Harris, known as La Tienda, that sells a huge range of imported Spanish delicacies (see Sources). Tim's work—alongside that of a growing number of importers and retailers—allows me to indulge one of my favorite ways to start or end a meal: a slice of Spanish cheese on a slice of green apple, topped with *dulce de membrillo* (quince compote).

Eggs occupy a special place in Spanish life. Wine- and sherry-makers used to clarify their wines with egg whites and then donate the egg yolks to the nuns. The result: dozens and dozens of pastry and dessert recipes that revolve around eggs. To this day in Andalucia, you can find extraordinary pastry stores run by nuns, selling wonderfully sweet, rich pastries. Some of the convents are closed to outsiders, so you have to buy your pastries through a small revolving door.

There are other testaments to the long-standing role that eggs have played in Spanish cooking. In 1618 Velasquez painted a classic picture of an old woman frying an egg in an earthenware pot. Back then, eggs were a sign of wealth; the more eggs you cooked, the greater the number of hens you possessed. So perhaps it's no surprise to find eggs in a huge variety of popular Spanish dishes, whether the comforting *tortilla de patatas* or a dish of fried eggs with chorizo sausage and garlic. Eggs transform even the simplest foods. For many Americans, eggs signify one meal: breakfast. But for Spaniards, eggs can be a part of every meal, from breakfast to dinner and tapas in between. As for me, I love nothing more than a pan-fried egg, with a gloriously runny yolk, a little salt, and lots of bread to wipe my plate clean.

In this chapter, and elsewhere in this book, you'll find recipes that use quail eggs. I love a great organic hen's egg, but quail eggs are a perfect match for tapas because of their size. My friend Didac López makes a fantastic tapa at his restaurant, La Estrella de Plata, in Barcelona: a deep-fried baby artichoke that has been stuffed with a quail egg, covered with caviar. I can only describe it in two words: un-believable.

Solomillo al Cabrales
Slow-roasted beef tenderloin with Cabrales cheese

Serves 4

1 pound beef tenderloin, in 1 piece

¼ cup Spanish extra-virgin olive oil, plus more for drizzling

1 bunch fresh thyme sprigs

Sea salt to taste

Black pepper to taste

3 ounces Cabrales cheese (see tips)

This is a classic dish, served in many restaurants in my home region of Asturias. The strong blue cheese is robust enough to stand up well alongside the beef. Here we aren't going to all the work of creating a sauce, but simply matching a great cheese with great-quality meat in its purest form.

Heat the oven to 200 degrees.

Using a brush, coat the tenderloin with the ¼ cup olive oil. Place the thyme in a small roasting pan and set the tenderloin on top. Roast until the temperature inside the tenderloin reaches 140 degrees on an instant-read thermometer; this should take around 40 minutes. Remove it from the oven. The tenderloin will be medium-rare at this stage.

Remove and discard the thyme. Place the roasting pan on a burner over high heat, and sear the tenderloin for 1 minute all over. Remove it from the heat, wrap it in aluminum foil, and let it rest for 5 minutes.

Cut the meat into 1-inch cubes, and arrange them on a warmed plate. Sprinkle each cube with sea salt and black pepper to taste. Place a piece of Cabrales cheese on top of each cube, and drizzle with olive oil. Serve immediately.

José's tips

Usually the searing of the meat is the first stage of a recipe. But technically, this doesn't make sense because the meat loses far too many juices. Slow cooking allows the juices to gel inside the meat. The searing at the end adds the caramelization that gives the extra flavor to the dish.

If you can't find Cabrales, use another Spanish blue cheese, such as Valdéon, or any other good blue cheese you can find.

Ensalada de manzanas con Murcia al vino
Apple and Murcia cheese salad with walnuts

Serves 4

1 Granny Smith apple, peeled, cored, and cut into ½-inch cubes

6 ounces Murcia al vino cheese (or any semi-hard goat cheese), cut into ½-inch cubes

½ tablespoon chopped chives

8 walnuts, shelled and chopped

¼ cup Spanish extra-virgin olive oil

2 tablespoons cider vinegar

Salt to taste

Cheese and apples is a classic combination—the fattiness of the cheese mixes so well with the juiciness and sweetness of the apple. Murcia, a goat's-milk cheese, is immersed in red wine for several days to make a very creamy cheese called Murcia al vino. It's often known here by its English name: drunken goat. The mix of the soft cheese with the crunchy apple and nuts works perfectly in this simple tapa.

Combine the apples, cheese, chives, and walnuts in a bowl. Add the oil and vinegar and mix together. Add salt to taste, and serve.

José's tips

You can cut the cheese into batons to make this salad more visually interesting. You can also vary the dressing by using sherry vinegar rather than the fruitier cider vinegar.

Marinated Idiazábal cheese with rosemary

Serves 4

3 garlic cloves

1 pound Idiazábal cheese (see tips), cut into 1-inch cubes

1 tablespoon black peppercorns

1 bay leaf

3 sprigs fresh rosemary

1 sprig fresh thyme

1¹/₂ cups Spanish extra-virgin olive oil

Idiazábal, the national cheese of the Basque country, is made from sheep's milk and is usually smoked, which gives it an unusual flavor and aroma. To many, it's the best cheese produced in Spain. This marinade makes the cheese very juicy and flavorful. It's a tapa that you see in many bars across Spain because it's simple to create and it keeps the cheese well.

Split open the garlic cloves by placing them on a chopping board and pressing down hard on them with the base of your hand or with the flat side of a knife.

Combine all the ingredients in a large bowl, coating the cheese thoroughly in the oil and herbs.

Cover the bowl and leave it overnight at room temperature. Spear the cheese cubes on toothpicks, and serve them on a plate.

José's tips

This would work well with any semi-hard cheese, if you can't find Idiazábal. Add any of your favorite herbs—chances are that it will be great.

Manchego cheese with Catalan tomato bread

Serves 4

2 large ripe tomatoes
(about ¼ pound)

4 slices rustic sourdough
bread, toasted

Spanish extra-virgin
olive oil to taste

Salt to taste

4 slices (about 2 ounces)
Manchego cheese

Manchego is quite simply the most popular regional cheese in Spain. It's also one of the most versatile: you can serve it as a cube on a toothpick, or thinly sliced on bread; it can be grated on top of a rice dish, or sliced to accompany *dulce de membrillo* (quince compote) as a dessert. Fortunately, it's also the most widely distributed Spanish cheese in America today, available on the shelves of many supermarkets. This simple tapa is a classic variation on *pan con tomate* (page 36).

The traditional way

Cut the tomatoes in half. Rub the open face of the tomatoes into the toast until the flesh is absorbed. Throw away the skin.

Drizzle the tomato-rubbed bread with olive oil—be as liberal with the oil as you like. Season to taste with salt. Place a slice of cheese on top, drizzle with a little more oil, and serve.

The modern way

Cut the tomatoes in half. Place a grater over a large mixing bowl. Rub the open face of the tomatoes onto the grater until all the flesh is grated. Throw away the skin.

Add the olive oil to the grated tomato (be liberal). Season to taste with salt.

Spoon the tomato-oil mixture onto the toast. Place a slice of cheese on top, drizzle with a little more oil, and serve.

"Mel i Matò"
Cheese and honey

Serves 4

¼ pound blanched almonds

2 tablespoons walnuts

½ cup sugar

¼ cup light Spanish olive oil

24 raspberries, rinsed

½ pound very fresh, unsalted, soft white cheese (such as a mature ricotta), cut into four ½-inch-thick slices

4 tablespoons honey

Katherine McLeod owns a creamery in Marshall, Virginia, where she makes a great selection of organic cheeses. My favorite is the simplest one—an unripe, fresh white cow's-milk cheese that my daughters love. It resembles Matò, the white cheese that the monks make in the monastery of Montserrat, where they clot the cheese with a special herb that grows in the mountains. (It's not just the cheese that makes this monastery exceptional: it also has one of the very few statues of a black Virgin Mary in Europe.) These mountains are home to some of the best honey in Europe, too.

Heat the oven to 200 degrees.

Place the almonds and walnuts on a baking sheet, and bake for 6 or 7 minutes. Remove the baking sheet from the oven, and using a rolling pin or the bottom of a heavy saucepan, break the nuts into big pieces. Set aside the walnuts and 12 almonds.

Combine the remaining almonds, the sugar, and the olive oil in a blender. Blend until you have a very fine sauce. Set it aside.

Place 12 of the raspberries in a fine-mesh sieve and set it over a bowl. Press on the berries with a spoon, extracting a fine puree, leaving only the seeds behind in the sieve. Discard the seeds.

To serve, drizzle a bit of the almond sauce and a bit of the raspberry puree in a zigzag on each plate. Place a slice of cheese in the center, and drizzle honey across the surface of the cheese to cover it. Sprinkle the reserved nuts on top. Arrange the remaining raspberries around the cheese, and serve.

José's tips

You can use any kind of berry—blueberries, for instance—instead of the raspberries here.

José's tips

Serve this with plenty of bread to dip into the oil and the soft egg yolk— the most satisfying part of this dish.

Huevos fritos con chorizo y patatas
Fried eggs with Spanish chorizo and potatoes

Serves 4

2 garlic cloves

3 tablespoons plus 1 cup Spanish extra-virgin olive oil

2 Idaho potatoes, peeled and cut into ¼-inch cubes

1 sprig fresh thyme

Salt to taste

2 chorizo sausages, cut into ¼-inch cubes

4 large eggs

Sea salt to taste

Eggs and chorizo is a classic combination; this modern twist includes potato and a touch of fresh thyme. The key to this tapa lies in the special yet simple technique of frying the eggs: by turning the egg in a small pan of hot olive oil, you create a wonderfully round shape that is crisp on the outside and soft on the inside. Once you fry eggs like this, you'll never go back to the flat, overcooked eggs you've fried before.

Split open the garlic cloves by placing them on a chopping board and pressing down hard on them with the base of your hand or with the flat side of a knife. Heat the 3 tablespoons of olive oil in a medium sauté pan over a medium flame. Add the garlic and cook for 1 minute, or until lightly browned. Add the potato cubes. Cook, shaking the pan in a circular motion every minute or so, until the potatoes are slightly browned, about 4 minutes. Add the sprig of thyme and sauté for another minute. Add salt to taste. Place the chorizo cubes in the pan, and continue to sauté, until slightly brown, 1 or 2 minutes. Set the pan aside.

In a small sauté pan, heat the remaining 1 cup of olive oil over a high flame to around 375 degrees (measured with a candy thermometer).

Crack 1 egg into a glass. Tip the sauté pan to a steep angle so the oil collects on one side to create a small bath. Carefully slide the egg into the hot oil. Using a wooden spoon, pour the oil over the egg 2 or 3 times. The egg will be ready in just 30 seconds. Transfer it to a plate with a slotted spoon, and season it with a little sea salt. Repeat with the remaining eggs, one at a time. You'll end up with round fried eggs, rather than the usual flat ones.

Cover a serving plate with the cubes of chorizo and potato. Place the eggs on top. Sprinkle with a little sea salt, and serve immediately.

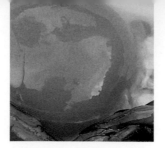

Revuelto de espárragos trigueros
Scrambled eggs with tender asparagus

Serves 4

8 green asparagus spears

2 tablespoons Spanish extra-virgin olive oil, plus more for drizzling

1 small spring onion, peeled and finely chopped

Salt to taste

2 large chicken eggs

1 tablespoon heavy cream

1 tablespoon chopped flat-leaf parsley

1 tablespoon butter

4 quail egg yolks

Sea salt to taste

This great breakfast tapa can be varied a dozen different ways—try it with mushrooms, scallions, or bacon. The fresh-tasting, slightly crunchy asparagus is a fantastic contrast to the creamy egg mixture, which I love to eat runny.

Cut off the asparagus tips and set them aside. Take the remaining stalks and break them with your hands—the stalks will break where the tough flesh meets the tender part of the asparagus. Discard the tough ends, and cut the tender part of the stalks lengthwise into very thin slices. Set aside.

Heat 1 tablespoon of the olive oil in a medium saucepan over a medium flame. Add the onions and sauté until translucent, about 2 minutes (be careful not to burn them).

When the onions are soft, add the asparagus tips and stalks, and salt to taste. Sauté for 2 minutes. Remove the pan from the heat and set it aside.

In a medium bowl, whisk the chicken eggs with the cream until the mixture is light and airy. Add the parsley and salt to taste.

Combine the remaining 1 tablespoon of olive oil and the butter in a sauté pan, and heat over a high flame until the butter starts to foam. Add the egg mixture, stir with a whisk, and cook for 30 seconds. The eggs will be cooked but runny and creamy.

Divide the eggs among 4 plates, and top with the asparagus-onion mixture. Place the raw quail egg yolk on top. Sprinkle with sea salt, drizzle with olive oil, and serve.

José's tips

If you don't like the idea of a raw quail egg yolk, you can always mix them into the chicken eggs in the pan (but do this off the heat). Just make sure you have some good bread nearby to soak up the runny eggs.

Flan al estilo de mi madre
Spanish flan in my mother's style

Serves 6

1 cup plus ³/₄ cup sugar

¹/₂ cup half-and-half

¹/₂ cup heavy cream

1 vanilla bean, split

1 strip lemon zest

1 cinnamon stick

3 large eggs

2 large egg yolks

My mother's flan is imperfect, but I love it. Like all good Spanish mothers, Marisa cooks her flan in an oven that gets too hot, creating small air bubbles in what should be a perfectly smooth and creamy dessert. Yet each of those bubbles takes me back to the Sunday lunches of my childhood, when my brothers and I would try to slurp up a flan in one glorious mouthful. This recipe is inspired by my mother's, but the results are even better.

Heat the oven to 275 degrees.

Prepare the caramel: Put the 1 cup sugar in a small pan. Start cooking it over low heat. After 5 or 6 minutes, you'll see the sugar starting to turn a light brown color. Cook for another 7 or 8 minutes, until it becomes dark brown. Keep stirring the caramel as it cooks; you don't want it to burn.

Remove the pan from the heat and carefully add ¹/₃ cup of warm water. The caramel will sputter and release steam as it hardens. Return the pan to low heat and cook until the caramel is thick and syrupy, about 5 minutes. Remove it from the heat and let it cool a little. Then coat the bottom and sides of 4 small ramekins with the caramel, using a spatula. Set the ramekins aside.

Combine the half-and-half and the cream in a medium saucepan. Add the vanilla bean and seeds, along with the lemon zest, cinnamon stick, and the remaining ³/₄ cup sugar. Bring to a boil over medium-high heat, removing the pan from the heat just as it reaches a boil.

In a large bowl, whisk together the eggs and egg yolks. Carefully pour the hot cream mixture into the eggs, whisking vigorously. Strain the mixture into another bowl; then fill the ramekins with the mixture.

Set the ramekins in a deep baking pan. Carefully fill the pan with enough hot water to reach halfway up the sides of the ramekins. Place the pan in the oven and bake for 45 minutes. Remove, and let the ramekins cool.

Store the flans in the refrigerator overnight. Serve cold.

José's tips

If you don't want to make a traditional caramel, use maple syrup. Cook good-quality maple syrup until it is reduced to a thick, dark brown consistency. Coat the ramekins just as you would with the caramel, and continue with the recipe.

Huevos de codorniz con huevas de trucha
Quail eggs with trout roe

Serves 4

For the dressing

2 tablespoons plain yogurt

1 tablespoon Spanish
extra-virgin olive oil

$\frac{1}{2}$ tablespoon sherry
vinegar

1 tablespoon chopped chives

Salt to taste

For the eggs

4 slices white bread,
crusts removed

1$\frac{1}{2}$ tablespoons Spanish
extra-virgin olive oil

8 quail eggs

Salt to taste

4 tablespoons trout roe
or salmon roe (see tips)

At my restaurants, people often ask me if this tapa is traditional. Well, it's not really. But bread and eggs are the staple of many diets around the world, Spain included. What we're doing here is presenting eggs and bread together in a very creative way. Remember: what's modern today will be traditional tomorrow.

Prepare the dressing: Mix the yogurt, olive oil, vinegar, and chives together in a small dish. Add salt to taste, and set it aside.

Using a 2-inch round cutter, cut a round from the center of each slice of bread. Set the slices aside, and discard the cut-out rounds.

Heat $\frac{1}{4}$ tablespoon of the olive oil in a nonstick frying pan over a medium flame. Brown 1 slice of bread on one side, about 1 minute. Turn the bread over. Place a drop of oil in the center hole, and crack 2 quail eggs into the hole. Add a touch of salt and cook for 1 minute, or until the white is just cooked, leaving the yolks runny. Using a spatula, carefully scoop the bread and eggs out of the pan and set them on a plate. Repeat with the remaining bread, oil, and quail eggs.

Spoon the trout roe onto the bread around the eggs, and spoon the yogurt dressing over the eggs. Serve immediately.

José's tips

You can replace the trout roe with anything your budget can afford, such as a top-quality Iranian caviar.

Tortilla de atún de almadrava
Tuna omelet with a twist

Serves 4

4 tablespoons olive oil from a can of tuna or anchovies

¼ large Spanish onion, peeled and thinly sliced

3 ounces fresh tuna (see tips)

Salt to taste

6 large eggs

2 tablespoons chopped chives

Sea salt to taste

Spanish extra-virgin olive oil, for drizzling

½ teaspoon chive flowers, optional, for garnish

My favorite *bocadillo*, or sandwich, to take to school was one my father would make early in the morning: good canned tuna in olive oil, cooked in an omelet. The omelet came with fresh tomato, between two slices of toast drizzled with olive oil. When I moved to the United States, I couldn't believe it was easier to find a great-quality fresh red tuna than a good canned version. Only recently have supermarkets begun to sell the best-quality Spanish tuna in a jar or can. So I started making this *tortilla* with fresh tuna, using the olive oil from a can of anchovies for its special aroma. It's an old flavor with a modern approach.

Heat 2 tablespoons of the olive oil from the tuna can in a small sauté pan over a medium flame. Add the onions and cook until soft and translucent, about 4 minutes. Remove the onions and set them aside.

Return the pan to the heat, raise it to high, and add 1 table-spoon of the oil. Add the tuna, season with salt to taste, and sear for 20 seconds on each side. Remove the tuna from the pan, cut it into ¼-inch-thick slices, and set them aside.

Break the eggs into a bowl and beat them lightly with a fork. Add 1 tablespoon of the chives, the reserved sautéed onions, and a little salt.

Pour one fourth of the egg mixture into the sauté pan and stir. Reduce the heat to low and cook for 1 minute. When the *tortilla* begins to set, transfer it to a plate; you want the top to be still runny. Repeat with the remaining eggs to make 3 more *tortillas*.

Serve the omelets runny side up, with slices of tuna on top. Sprinkle a little sea salt over each tuna slice. Drizzle a little extra-virgin olive oil over the whole plate, sprinkle with the remaining chopped chives and chive flowers, and serve immediately.

José's tips

If you don't want to be so adventurous, buy good-quality canned tuna to substitute for the fresh tuna—that is how I've always done it. Just make sure you get a really high quality canned tuna, preferably a Spanish one.

You can serve this *tortilla* with the eggs runny, or you can flip it with the help of a plate and cook it for another minute before topping it with the tuna.

fish

chapter 12

capitulo 12

Recipes	Wine tips
Merluza en salsa verde con almejas "Juan Mari Arzak" Hake in green sauce "Arzak"	Lusco from the Rias Baixas region (Alvariño grape)
Caldo de pescado Traditional fish stock	Fillaboa from the Rias Baixas region (Alvariño grape)
Rape con romesco Monkfish with romesco sauce	Clos Martinez from the Priorat region (Garnacha/Cabernet Sauvignon grapes)
Besugo a la sal American red snapper baked in salt	Milmanda from the Conca de Barbera region (Chardonnay grape)
Lubina a la donostiarra Rockfish with guindilla pepper, vinegar, and garlic	Aurus from the Rioja region (Tempranillo grape)
Fritura de pescado Flounder fried in the traditional way	Manzanilla "La Gitana" from the Jerez region (Palomino grape)
Salmón al estilo de Asturias Asturian-style salmon	Pujanza "Norte" from the Rioja region (Tempranillo grape)
Huevas de pescado en vinagreta Hudson shad roe with Spanish olive oil and sherry vinegar	Jane Ventura Brut Natural from the Cava region (Xarello/Macabeo/Parellada grapes)

pescado

Nothing excites Spanish appetites quite as much as fish. Spanish fish markets are amazing, even in the smallest towns, and a freshly caught fish can bring a smile to the face of the most accomplished chef. I once saw Pedro Subijana, a two-star Michelin chef, walking out of his restaurant late at night with a big grin under his handlebar moustache—he was going home with a green plastic bag filled with three fresh squid that a fisherman had just caught. The most amazing array of fresh fish—the one that inspires chefs and home cooks alike—is the one at the heart of my beloved market in Barcelona, la Boquería. At the center of the market, in a circle of ice-drenched stands, is a sparkling display of silvers, blues, reds, and pinks—every edible treasure that comes from the sea. I'll never forget one trip to la Boquería with my friend Rick Tramonto, from Tru in Chicago. We bought one of everything, spending more than $1,000 on an eclectic sea-catch (many of them still alive and kicking), which we packed into three huge coolers. There were baby octopuses, *gambas* from Palamós (unarguably the best shrimp in the world), hake, razor clams, and sea cucumbers (which are unique to Catalonia). We started cooking at 7:00 in the evening and were still going at 2:00 in the morning.

When Spanish people visit the United States, one of the first things they say is that the fish here is not as tasty as it is back home. I must beg to differ. America's coastlines also produce wonderful fish, and with so many ethnic groups here, you can find sensational ethnic fish markets. For instance, in the otherwise modest town of Centreville, Virginia, there are fantastic Korean markets; similarly, you can find extraordinary Portuguese markets in New Jersey. I buy the freshest sea urchins, hake, and monkfish—equal to anything you can find in Spain—at A&H in Bethesda, Maryland, a store owned by two Spaniards, my friends Alfonso and Herminio Martinez. Today you can even buy *angulas,* or baby eels, a quintessential Spanish delicacy, from Maine. With the help of these ethnic markets and specialist suppliers, you can reproduce the most traditional Spanish dishes in America—and with a little imagination, create a few new ones of your own.

Merluza en salsa verde con almejas "Juan Mari Arzak"

Hake in green sauce "Arzak"

Serves 4

8 Manila clams

2 tablespoons Spanish extra-virgin olive oil

1 small garlic clove, peeled and finely chopped

Pinch of all-purpose flour

Salt to taste

¹⁄₂ pound hake (see tips), skin on, cut into 4 pieces

1 tablespoon finely chopped parsley

1¹⁄₂ tablespoons crisp white wine, such as an Albariño from Galicia

The modern revolution in Spanish cooking started with a handful of Basque chefs who were willing to make a statement. Their leader was Juan Mari Arzak, who owns the three-Michelin-star restaurant Arzak in San Sebastián. This dish represents the best of Basque cooking, and the best is Juan Mari.

Bring 1 quart of water to a boil in a large pot. Add 4 clams to the boiling water and cook for 5 to 10 seconds, until you see them just opening a fraction. Remove the clams from the water, and repeat with the remaining 4 clams. Holding them over a bowl to collect the juices, take the clams out of the shells with the help of a paring knife. Set aside both the clams and the juices.

In a small terra-cotta or metal casserole that's just big enough to hold the fish snugly, heat the olive oil over a low flame. Add the garlic and cook until it seems to dance in the oil, but don't let it brown at all, about 45 seconds. Add the flour.

Sprinkle some salt over the fish and place it, skin side down, in the casserole. Add the parsley. Shaking the casserole in a circular motion, or moving the pieces around with a spoon in a circular motion, cook for 3 to 4 minutes. Turn the hake over, and repeat the same process. You want to warm the fish very slowly at a low temperature.

Add the clams, the clam juices, and the wine. Cook for another 4 minutes, without ever allowing the liquid to boil. The natural gelatins of the fish will emulsify with the oil, making a subtle, light green sauce. Add salt to taste, and serve immediately.

José's tips

You can use codfish if you can't find hake. Remember to maintain a low cooking temperature throughout: the low heat and continuous motion allow the oil, wine, and natural juices to emulsify into this delicate sauce.

Caldo de pescado
Traditional fish stock

Makes 1½ quarts

Bones of 1 whole
red snapper (see tips),
including the head,
washed well

4 sprigs fresh parsley

1 Spanish onion, peeled and
halved

1 leek, well washed, outer
leaves removed

3 tablespoons Spanish
extra-virgin olive oil

1 cup dry white wine

In all the fish restaurants along the coast of Spain, fish stock is the common denominator. The *caldo de pescado* is used for fish soup, to make paella, and to form the base for many traditional fish stews.

Place 3 quarts of water in a stockpot, add the fish bones, and bring to a boil. Using a ladle, remove the white foam that forms on the surface (this will give you a cleaner, clearer stock).

Reduce the heat to low and add the remaining ingredients, including the oil and wine. Simmer for 25 to 30 minutes, skimming the surface of the stock if any more foam appears.

Remove the pot from the heat and let the stock rest for 10 minutes; then strain it. Keep it in the refrigerator for up to 1 week or in the freezer until you need to use it.

José's tips

You can substitute rockfish for the red snapper, but don't use a blue fish like tuna. If fish bones aren't available at all, buy 1 pound of mussels and simmer them for just 4 or 5 minutes with the other ingredients; you'll end up with a stock that has a wonderful flavor of the sea.

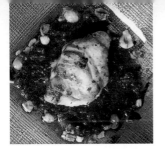

Rape con romesco
Monkfish with romesco sauce

Serves 4

1 pound monkfish fillet

6 bay leaves

2 tablespoons Spanish extra-virgin olive oil, plus more for drizzling

Salt to taste

White pepper to taste

1 recipe Romesco (page 95)

Traditionally, *romesco* was a fish stew made by sailors from the catch of the day. Today *romesco* has become a sauce by itself, served at room temperature to accompany any vegetable or even meat. Here it's used with monkfish, but you can use any meaty fish to create a *romesco*-based masterpiece.

Examine the monkfish to see if any bits of membrane remain. If they do, remove them carefully. Using a sharp knife, make 6 incisions about 1 inch apart in the fillet; do not cut all the way through. Slip a bay leaf into each incision.

Heat the 2 tablespoons olive oil in a large sauté pan over a medium-high flame. Add the monkfish and cook it on each side until lightly browned, 3 to 4 minutes. Set the fish aside to cool.

When the monkfish is cool, slice the fillet all the way through to create 1-inch-thick medallions. Season with salt and white pepper to taste. Spoon a bed of *romesco* sauce onto a plate. Place the medallions on top, drizzle with olive oil, and serve.

José's tips
You can add extra oil to the romesco and serve it as a dressing on a mesclun salad, with the fish on the side. It makes for a great salad entrée.

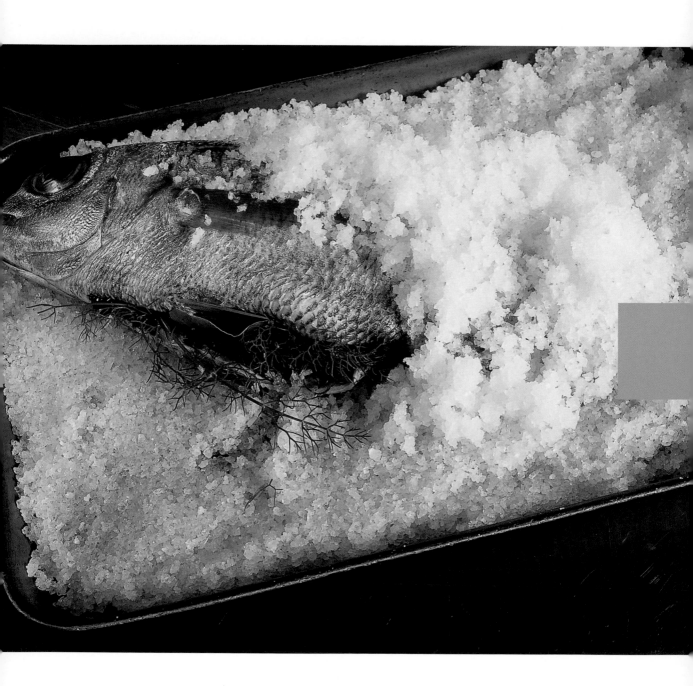

Besugo a la sal
American red snapper baked in salt

Serves 4

3 pounds kosher salt

1 red snapper
(approximately 2½ pounds;
see tips), gutted
but not scaled

3 fresh bay leaves

Sea salt to taste

¼ cup Spanish
extra-virgin olive oil

1 tablespoon sherry vinegar

This technique is the easiest way to cook a whole fish—and to surprise people in the process. It captures the moist, juicy flavor that you can get only by cooking a whole fish. Inside the salt casing, the fish cooks perfectly, giving your guests a spectacularly fresh (not salty) taste.

Heat the oven to 375 degrees.

In a large bowl, mix the kosher salt with 1½ cups of water. You want a damp paste that you can mold with your hands. Spread half of the salt paste over the bottom of a baking dish and place the red snapper on top of it. Turn the upper fins to the side and place the bay leaves inside the belly. Cover the fish completely with the remaining salt.

Bake for 27 minutes. Remove the baking dish from the oven and let the salt-encased fish rest for 5 minutes. Then, using a fork and spoon, crack open the side of the salt crust. The upper half of the salt (now a hard shell) should lift off easily.

Using a knife, cut below the head to the bone. Cut along the spine. With the help of a fork, remove the skin. What lies underneath is the juicy meat of the red snapper. Using a knife, lift the meat off the bone. Sprinkle with a little sea salt, the olive oil, and the sherry vinegar. Serve immediately.

José's tips

You can use striped bass or rockfish instead of the red snapper; these are the only other types of fish I recommend. A 3-pound fish takes 30 minutes in the oven. These temperatures and times are very precise. After you make this dish a few times; you'll discover the perfect settings for your own oven.

Lubina a la donostiarra
Rockfish with guindilla pepper, vinegar, and garlic

Serves 4

3 tablespoons Spanish extra-virgin olive oil

1 garlic clove, peeled and thinly sliced

1 guindilla chili pepper (or your favorite dried chili pepper), halved

½ pound rockfish fillet (see tips)

1 teaspoon sherry vinegar

½ teaspoon chopped flat-leaf parsley

Salt to taste

This dish is very traditional in the Basque country, where the fish is cooked on charcoal, then filleted and covered with chili pepper, vinegar, and garlic. This type of garnish is called *donostiarra,* which refers to the San Sebastián area of the Basque country. Cooking a whole fish on charcoal is not for everyone; this adaptation is far simpler and quicker. It comes from Lluis Cruanyes, who was one of the best restaurateurs in Spain in the 1990s. Lluis, who gave me my first break in New York, used to call this technique "Robespierre," in honor of the infamous leader of the French Revolution. I guess he was thinking of the thin slices.

Heat a salamander or broiler to a high temperature.

In a small sauté pan, heat 2 tablespoons of the olive oil over a medium flame. Add the garlic slices and cook until slightly brown, about 1 minute (make sure that you don't burn the garlic). Add the chili pepper and remove the pan from the heat. Set it aside.

Coat the bottom of a baking dish with the remaining 1 tablespoon of olive oil. Using a sharp knife, cut the fish into diagonal slices no more than ¼-inch thick. Lay the slices in the oiled dish without overlapping.

Place the baking dish under the salamander or broiler for no more than 1 minute—just enough to cook the fish but keep it moist. Remove it from the heat and sprinkle the sherry vinegar over the fish. Cover with the garlic mixture and its oil. Sprinkle with the parsley, add salt to taste, and serve immediately.

José's tips

You can use Dover sole, flounder, or even salmon. You can pre-slice the fish and keep it in the refrigerator so the slices are ready to cook in next to no time.

Fritura de pescado
Flounder fried in the traditional way

Serves 4

1 quart Spanish
extra-virgin olive oil

1 whole flounder
(1 pound; see tips), scaled

Salt to taste

White pepper to taste

2 cups all-purpose flour

1 lemon, quartered

Frying is the ultimate cooking technique in Andalucia, the land of olive trees, olives, and olive oil. I did my military service in the Spanish navy in Cádiz, at the southern tip of Spain, where I was able to see the wonders of frying at first hand. My favorite was a sandwich of fried squid with mayonnaise, which we bought when we had no money to spend on anything else. Five years ago, with the help of my good friend Carles Abellàn, I went to a tiny restaurant called Alhucemas in Sanlucar la Mayor, outside Seville. For three or four hours we ate the best fried seafood and shellfish I had ever tasted. Right there I understood the importance of standing up for the much-maligned technique of frying—something I hadn't enjoyed as much since I was a sailor, many years before.

In a small deep pot, heat the oil to 350 degrees (measured with a candy thermometer).

While the oil is heating, cut off the head of the fish. Cutting across the spine, slice the fish into 1½-inch-wide pieces. Place the slices on paper towels to absorb any extra moisture. Season each piece, including the head and tail, with plenty of salt and a bit of white pepper.

Put the flour on a plate and dip both sides of the fish pieces in the flour. Shake off any excess.

Put 2 pieces of fish in the oil, being careful not to let it splash. You'll see bubbles and hear the crackling noise of the frying. After 1 minute, turn the fish over. Fry for another minute, until the fish is golden, and then remove the pieces from the oil. Place them on paper towels to absorb any excess oil. Wait 30 seconds between batches to make sure the oil returns to 350 degrees, and repeat with the remaining fish.

Reassemble the fish on the plate. Serve immediately, with the lemon slices.

José's tips

If you can't find flounder, you can substitute striped bass or rockfish. And if you don't want to cut the fish yourself, ask your fish supplier to prepare it as described. If you're good with chopsticks, use them to turn the fish in the oil—it's almost like cooking tempura, which has a lot in common with the Spanish *fritura.* There shouldn't be much excess oil on the cooked fish pieces; they should be just crisp on the outside and moist on the inside.

Salmón al estilo de Asturias
Asturian-style salmon

Serves 4

¼ pound center-cut salmon (preferably Copper River), skinned

2 Golden Delicious apples

2½ tablespoons Spanish extra-virgin olive oil

½ tablespoon unsalted butter

Salt to taste

1 tablespoon cider vinegar

3 juniper berries

1 ounce salmon roe

1 ounce Cabrales cheese (or any other good blue cheese), cut into small cubes

1 tablespoon chopped chives

Sea salt to taste

José's tips

If you don't like raw fish, you can cover the salmon with the dressing and place it in a small pan under a salamander or broiler for a few seconds to cook it slightly, before serving it with the apple puree, cheese, and chives. Or you could always do the same dish with smoked salmon.

Asturias, the region where I was born, is the most beautiful part of Spain (to me, at least): the sea, the mountains, the fish, the cheeses, the apples, the chestnuts. The king of Asturian gastronomy is the wild salmon that swims up rivers like the Sella to lay its eggs. My uncle Gélin lives in Naves, one of the smallest and prettiest towns anywhere. Gélin, like my grandfather Ramón, is an avid fisherman. Every year he waits anxiously for wild salmon season to open. The fishing is so strictly limited now that you have to enter a lottery to get permission to fish on just a handful of days in a small part of the river. When Gélin catches a salmon (which is rare, given their scarcity), it's a day of joy and celebration. This dish is not a traditional dish in the region, but it features four of the main ingredients in Asturian food—salmon, apples, cider, and Cabrales cheese.

Heat the oven to 325 degrees.

Cut the salmon into ¼-inch cubes. Put the cubes on a plate, cover with plastic wrap, and refrigerate.

Place one of the apples on a square of aluminum foil with ½ tablespoon of the olive oil and the butter. Wrap it up in the foil and bake until it softens, approximately 20 minutes. Remove the foil and let the apple cool slightly. Then remove the skin and the core. Put the apple on a plate, and using a fork, mash it to form a puree. Add salt to taste and set it aside.

Peel the other apple and cut into ¼-inch cubes, and place them in a bowl.

In a small bowl, mix the cider vinegar with the remaining 2 tablespoons of olive oil and a little salt. Smash the juniper berries with the flat side of a knife and add them to the dressing.

Add the salmon cubes to the dressing and allow to marinate for 10 minutes; then remove the salmon, reserving the dressing.

Spread a thin layer of the apple puree on a serving plate. Place the marinated salmon cubes on top. Cover with the fresh apple cubes and salmon roe, and sprinkle the cheese over that. Drizzle with the dressing, sprinkle with the chives, add sea salt to taste, and serve.

Huevas de pescado en vinagreta
Hudson shad roe with Spanish olive oil and sherry vinegar

Serves 4

1 set shad roe (about ½ pound; see tips)

1 tablespoon salt, plus more to taste

1 ripe plum tomato

¼ cup Spanish extra-virgin olive oil

2 tablespoons sherry vinegar

½ green bell pepper, seeded and cut into small cubes

½ red bell pepper, seeded and cut into small cubes

1 shallot, peeled and finely chopped

1 tablespoon chopped chives

If there's one thing that epitomizes American seasonal ingredients, it's shad roe. Each spring it shows up at the fish markets without fail. In Spain we love to eat the roe of different fish, but to me shad roe is the quintessential American fish ingredient. Here it's used as a New World flavor prepared in an Old World way. Refreshingly simple.

Wash the shad roe carefully under cool water, making sure you don't break the membrane.

Bring 2 cups of water to a boil in a medium pan, and add the 1 tablespoon of salt. Place the shad roe in the water and boil for 30 seconds. Then cover the pan, remove it from the heat, and set it aside for 3 minutes. At this point the shad roe should be half-cooked, with the inside still pink. Remove it from the water and set it aside. (If you prefer the shad roe to be cooked more fully, leave it in the water for a few more minutes.)

Cut an X in the bottom of the tomato with a sharp knife. Place the tomato in a large bowl of fresh hot water for 10 seconds. Drain, and remove the skins and seeds. Cut the flesh into ¼-inch cubes.

Mix the oil and vinegar together in a medium bowl, and season with salt to taste. Add the bell pepper cubes, the tomato cubes, and the shallots, and toss.

Cut the shad roe into ½-inch-thick slices. Arrange them on a plate and cover them with the dressing. Sprinkle with the chives, add salt to taste, and serve.

José's tips

Look for shad roe that is a nice deep red color. It comes in pairs, but you'll need only one set for this tapa. Once it is cooked, you can remove the membrane if you prefer. And if you don't like shad roe, or can't find it, you can use the same dressing with cooked shrimp or crabmeat.

shellfish

chapter 13

capitulo 13

Recipe

Mejillones al vapor
Mussels steamed in their own juices

Calamares en su tinta
Squid in its own ink

Bogavante a la gallega
Galician-style lobster with pimentón and olive oil

Txangurro
Basque-style stuffed Maryland blue crabs

Almejas en salsa verde a la moderna
Clams in green sauce, modern-style

Ensalada de mejillones en vinagreta de tomate
Mussels salad with a tomato vinaigrette

Fritura de cangrejo blando
Softshell crabs fried in extra-virgin olive oil

Rossejat
Pan-fried angel hair pasta with shrimp

Wine tips

Emilio Rojo from the Ribeiro region
(Treixadura grape)

Tras Lanzas from the Cigales region
(Tempranillo grape)

Gramona Imperial Brut Gran Reserva from the
Cava region (Xarello/Macabeo/Parellada grapes)

Txomín Etxaniz from the Chacoli de Getaria
region (Hondarrabi Zuri grape)

Morgadio from the Rias Baixas region
(Alvariño grape)

Gran Feudo Rosado from the Navarra region
(Garnacha grape)

Viña Godebal from the Valdeorras region
(Godello grape)

Viña Sol from the Penedes region
(Parellada grape)

mariscos

All across Spain, you can find people arguing over which *gambas* (shrimp) are the tastiest. That poses some problems for those of us cooking Spanish tapas here in America, because it's hard to find exactly the same species of shellfish that live off the Spanish coast. Over the years, I've been able to import some of the creatures that are so characteristic of Spanish cuisine, like *cigalas* (Norwegian lobster) or *carabineros,* the tasty, giant red shrimp. Sadly, they're not available to most American cooks. But there are some wonderful shellfish here that make perfectly good substitutes, such as the Chesapeake's blue crabs, which I use to make *txangurro,* a very popular crabmeat stew from the Basque country. For the light and flavorful *mejillones al vapor,* I use Prince Edward Island mussels, which are actually sweeter than the ones we have in Spain. Then there are the amazing softshell crabs from the East Coast. From local octopus and baby squid to Gulf of Mexico shrimp, the huge range of American shellfish can help any cook create authentic Spanish tapas at home.

For years I've been defending the quality of American seafood for one simple reason: Its quality is amazing. But it doesn't matter how good your shellfish is if you overcook it. Even the best, freshest shellfish can be easily ruined by a few extra seconds. Mussels need to be cooked only until they open; lobsters until the meat is translucent. Clams only need to be warmed up; if they are cooked too long, they become chewy and lose their pristine, ocean-fresh flavor.

There's nothing I love more than grilling fresh shellfish like *cigalas,* but it's not the only way to taste the best shellfish. In a tiny bar called Quimet i Quimet, on a side street in a residential neighborhood of Barcelona, you can eat some of the finest seafood anywhere in the world—and it's straight from the can. This is where my friend Quim Pérez makes the most incredible selection of tapas in the smallest of kitchen spaces, behind the bar. Among the selections of tuna and peppers, or caviar and escabeche, there's one of the best tapas I know: a plate of white clams in their juices, simply poured out of a can. Apart from being an extraordinary tapas chef, Quim prides himself on finding the very best preserved foods, especially cans of shellfish. With their soft texture, sweet taste, and unmistakable aroma of the sea, Quim's clams are what canned foods should be: the best ingredients kept for when you really need them.

Fortunately you don't have to be in Barcelona to eat them. Check out the suppliers in the Sources section to explore the range of top-quality canned seafood you can buy in the U.S.

Mejillones al vapor
Mussels steamed in their own juices

Serves 4

2 tablespoons Spanish
extra-virgin olive oil

1 pound (about 24) Prince
Edward Island mussels,
cleaned thoroughly

1 fresh bay leaf

Sea salt to taste

To me, the best part of eating mussels is when you reach the bottom of the pan. It's only when you dip your spoon in the deliciously briny juices that you really savor the essence of mussels. In fact, the taste of good mussels can drive me to great lengths. As a young cook at el Bulli, I remember getting into a small boat on the beach close to the restaurant to go fishing for little rock mussels in April. Whether or not the menu offered mussels depended on how successful we were at sea. Things have changed a lot at el Bulli since those days, 15 years ago.

Heat the olive oil in a medium pot over a high flame. Add the mussels and bay leaf. You'll hear a crackling noise of the water as the wet mussels hit the oil. Cover the pot with a tight-fitting lid.

Shaking the pan every 10 seconds or so, cook just until the shells open, no more than 40 seconds; the mussels will have steamed in their own juices. Add sea salt to taste and serve immediately, with plenty of bread to dunk into the juices.

José's tips

There is no better way to eat mussels than in their own natural juices, with nothing added, allowing their natural flavor to shine through. But if you feel creative, you can add some chives, a touch of lemon juice, white wine—or even a teaspoon of mustard. Just remember: more often than not, simplicity is the key to success.

Calamares en su tinta
Squid in its own ink

Serves 4

1 pound squid (see tips), cleaned

3 tablespoons Spanish extra-virgin olive oil

2 Spanish onions, peeled and thinly sliced (about 2 cups)

1 garlic clove, peeled

1 bay leaf

1/4 green bell pepper (about 3 ounces), seeded and sliced into small strips

1/4 cup dry white wine

1/4 cup canned whole tomatoes with juice, pureed

1 cup Traditional Fish Stock (page 184) or water

3 teaspoons squid ink (see tips)

Salt to taste

José's tips

Go to your local fish market and tell them that you want whole fresh squid—they'll be able to get them for you. It makes a huge difference. Frozen squid aren't bad, but they don't give the same flavor to this dish. If the squid is whole and fresh, you can find the ink inside the squid in a tiny sac. In any case, many fish markets sell the ink, already prepared, in plastic bags.

When I was a kid, no moment was more fun for me than when my parents came back from the fish market on Saturdays with a squid or cuttlefish. Besides the funny look of the squid to any child's eye, the really fascinating part came when we were cleaning them. We'd find all kinds of fish in their bellies—we couldn't believe that such a tiny mouth could eat such big fish. I've bought lots of fresh squid in America, but I've found a fish in its belly only once or twice. Is the ocean really running out of fish, or do the Mediterranean squid have a bigger appetite?

If the squid bodies are small (say 2 to 3 inches in length), leave them whole. If they are larger, cut them into 1-inch rings. Or if you prefer, cut them into triangles by cutting the side of the body lengthwise, laying the squid out flat, and slicing diagonally across to make a series of triangle shapes.

Pour the olive oil into a small flameproof casserole and bring to medium heat. Add the onions, garlic, bay leaf, and bell peppers, and cook, stirring occasionally, until the onions caramelize, about 30 minutes. You'll know the onions are caramelized when they are soft, tender, and light brown in color. If the onions begin to get too dark, add 1/2 tablespoon of water. This will help the onions to cook evenly without burning.

Add the wine and cook until reduced by half, about 1 minute. Pour in the tomato puree and cook for another 5 minutes, or until the tomato has reduced and become a nice deep red color. Pour in the fish stock (or water) and bring to a simmer. Add the squid ink, stir together, and remove from the heat.

Take out the bay leaf and discard it. Using a hand blender, puree the sauce until it is smooth and thoroughly mixed together.

Return the casserole to medium heat. Season the squid with salt and add it to the casserole. Cook until the squid is soft, 15 to 20 minutes. Serve immediately.

Bogavante a la gallega
Galician-style lobster with pimentón and olive oil

Serves 4

1 Idaho potato, peeled and cut into ½-inch cubes

¼ cup sea salt, plus more to taste

¼ cup Spanish extra-virgin olive oil, plus more for drizzling

1 bay leaf

1 teaspoon black peppercorns

1 Maine lobster (about 1½ pounds)

1 teaspoon *pimentón* (Spanish sweet paprika)

This dish is inspired by the classic *pulpo a la gallega,* which is a very simple dish of boiled octopus sprinkled with *pimentón,* olive oil, and sea salt. It exemplifies the simplicity of northern Spanish cooking. Here I use lobster—a genuine American ingredient—which is much quicker to cook than the octopus. In fact, it's important to watch the cooking time closely, to prevent the lobster from becoming rubbery.

Bring 2 quarts of water to a boil in a medium pot. Add the potato cubes, ¼ cup sea salt, ¼ cup olive oil, bay leaf, and peppercorns. Boil for 8 minutes, or until the potatoes are soft. Add the lobster to the pot and cook for 4 minutes.

Remove the potatoes and the lobster from the pot and drain them. Crack the lobster claws and cut the tail into 6 medallions.

Arrange the lobster and potatoes on a serving dish. Place the *pimentón* in a fine-mesh sieve, and tapping the side of the sieve gently to break up any large chunks, sprinkle the *pimentón* evenly over the top. Sprinkle with a little sea salt, drizzle with olive oil, and serve.

José's tips
You can use this technique with crabs, shrimp, or even monkfish cut into big chunks.

Txangurro
Basque-style stuffed Maryland blue crabs

Serves 4

For the crabs

2 tablespoons sea salt

8 fresh blue crabs (see tips), preferably female (about 2½ pounds total, to yield ⅓ pound of meat)

For the filling

6 ripe tomatoes

2 tablespoons Spanish extra-virgin olive oil

1 garlic clove, peeled and finely chopped

½ Spanish onion, peeled and finely chopped

½ leek, white part only, well washed and finely chopped

1 guindilla chili pepper (or your favorite dried chili pepper)

2 tablespoons Spanish brandy

¼ cup Txacoli (a Basque white wine) or other fresh, young white wine

6 fresh tarragon leaves

Salt to taste

This tapa is based on a fairly modern Basque-country dish, which has become very much a part of the mainstream. Basque people love their crabs, and *txangurro* has grown into something of a national dish in the region. For me, the most frustrating part of preparing this dish is that I rarely finish making it. Why? Because I love to eat the meat as I'm cleaning the crabs.

Cook the crabs: Bring 3 quarts of water to a boil in a large pot and add the sea salt. When the water is boiling, drop in the crabs and cook for 8 minutes. Drain, and allow the crabs to cool. Then remove the claws and legs, taking care to keep the upper shell intact. Working over a bowl to collect the juices, remove the meat from the claws, legs, and body. Reserve the juices and the crabmeat. Carefully clean and set aside 4 of the empty shells.

Prepare the filling: Cut each tomato in half lengthwise. Place a grater over a bowl and grate the open side of the tomatoes into the bowl. Discard the skin. Strain the grated flesh through a sieve to produce 2 cups of tomato puree. Set it aside.

Heat the olive oil in a medium pan over a medium flame. When the oil is hot, add the garlic and cook until it begins to brown a little, about 30 seconds. Add the onions and cook for 2 minutes. Add the leeks and the guindilla, reduce the heat to low, and cook until the onions are soft and translucent, about 15 minutes.

Add the brandy and the wine, and cook until reduced by half, about 1 minute. Add the tomato puree and cook until it thickens and begins to darken in color, about 5 minutes.

Remove the pan from the heat and add the crabmeat. Add the crab juices and the tarragon. Stir to combine, and add salt to taste.

To serve, place an empty crab shell on each plate. Fill the shells with the crabmeat mixture. Serve with a teaspoon on the side.

José's tips

If your time is limited you can buy crabs already cleaned and boiled. Just make sure that they have not been seasoned and are very fresh. If you can't find Maryland blue crabs, you can always substitute Dungeness crabs from the West Coast.

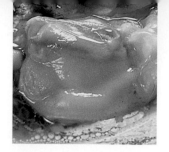

Almejas en salsa verde a la moderna
Clams in green sauce, modern-style

Serves 4

20 Manila clams, cleaned thoroughly

1 tablespoon finely chopped flat-leaf parsley

3 tablespoons Spanish extra-virgin olive oil

2 tablespoons very finely chopped Spanish onion

½ garlic clove, very finely chopped (about ¼ tablespoon)

1 tablespoon dry white wine

Salt to taste

Salsa verde, or green sauce, is a Basque-country classic, usually served with hake or salt cod. Here I've updated the sauce and served it with clams to simplify the dish and make it more subtle. This recipe emphasizes the purity of the clams and avoids the common mistake of making them chewy.

Bring 1 quart of water to a boil in a large pot. Add 4 clams to the boiling water and cook just until you see them opening a fraction, 5 to 10 seconds. Then immediately remove them. Repeat with the remaining clams.

Place a strainer over a bowl to collect the juices. Working over the bowl, use a knife to make two incisions on the side of each clam shell to break the muscle, being careful not to break the clam itself. Open the shell and separate the clam from the shell, using the knife or a teaspoon. Carefully put the shelled clams in the strainer. At this point you should have around ¼ cup of clam juices.

Put the parsley and the collected clam juices in a blender and blend until it forms a very fine puree. You should have a nice green sauce. Set it aside.

Heat the olive oil in a medium sauté pan over a medium flame. Add the onions and cook until soft and translucent, about 3 minutes (do not let them brown). Add the garlic and wine, and cook until the wine evaporates, 20 seconds. Add 2 tablespoons of the parsley sauce and cook for 1 minute. The result should be a very light sauce. Season with salt to taste.

To serve, place the clams in a soup plate and cover them with the sauce.

José's tips
This is the best technique for cooking clams, oysters, or any shellfish to ensure that you don't overcook them, which makes them chewy.

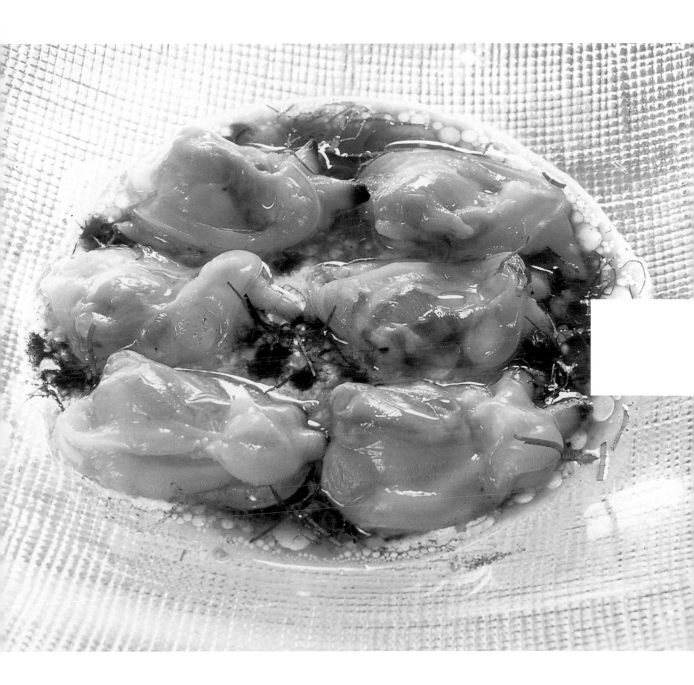

Ensalada de mejillones en vinagreta de tomate
Mussel salad with a tomato vinaigrette

For the dressing

1 ripe plum tomato

3 tablespoons Spanish extra-virgin olive oil

½ tablespoon sherry vinegar

Salt to taste

For the mussels

½ pound (about 15) Prince Edward Island mussels

1 garlic clove, peeled

1 cup parsley, with stems

Salt to taste

In the northern Mediterranean coast town of Rosas—next to Cadaqués, where the great Salvador Dalí lived, created, and died—the seawater is clean and the coastline was once covered with small white mussels called *mejillones de roca,* or rock mussels. Those mussels, which are now quite scarce, are salty, juicy, and very flavorful. Prince Edward Island mussels are cultivated, and they're not as salty as the ones I remember from Spain, but they are almost the same size, look very much like the Spanish ones, and are easy to find here.

Bring 2 cups of water to a boil in a small saucepan. Fill a medium bowl with ice water. Drop the tomato into the boiling water and blanch it for 10 seconds. Then drain it immediately and immerse it in the ice water to halt the cooking process. When it has cooled slightly, remove the skin, cut the firm flesh into small cubes, and set them aside. Set aside the softer flesh from inside the tomato for use in preparing the dressing. To make the dressing, take 2 tablespoons of the soft tomato flesh and place it in a cup. Add the oil and the vinegar and mix together using a hand blender. Add salt to taste and set aside.

Bring 1 quart of water to a boil in a large pot. Add 4 mussels and cook just until they open, 10 to 15 seconds. Remove them from the pot and repeat with the remaining mussels. Set a strainer over a bowl. Working over the bowl to collect the juices, use a knife to make two incisions on the side of each shell to break the muscle, being careful not to break the mussel itself. Open the shell and remove the mussel, using the knife or a tea-spoon. Carefully put the mussels in the strainer to collect their juices. At this point you should have around ¼ cup of mussel juices. Set the mussels aside.

Put the garlic and parsley into a cup and add the reserved mussel juices. Use a hand blender to mix together into a puree. Add a little salt to taste, and set aside.

Cover the bottom of a soup plate with the tomato dressing. Place the mussels on top of the dressing. Spoon a little of the parsley-garlic mixture around the mussels. Sprinkle the firm tomato cubes on top, and serve.

José's tips

If you want to refine this, you can add 4 tomato-seed "fillets" from the plum tomato (page 40).

You can also serve the mussels on the half shell, covering them with the tomato dressing and parsley sauce. It's great finger food.

Fritura de cangrejo blando
Softshell crabs fried in extra-virgin olive oil

Serves 4

3 cups Spanish
extra-virgin olive oil

2 medium softshell crabs

Salt to taste

White pepper to taste

½ cup all-purpose flour

1 large egg, whisked

½ cup breadcrumbs

1 lemon, quartered

To me, the softshell crab is the most unique ingredient America has to offer. When the warm weather arrives, the blue crabs begin to molt, starting in Florida and moving north up the Eastern Seaboard. For a few magical hours, after they shed their old hard shell, the crabs are soft and silky and very exposed to predators. At that moment they are caught, the shell-hardening process stops, and softshells show up on menus across the country. The ones I prefer are the smallest, which I find to be the sweetest of all. You can almost eat them in two bites, and they happen to be the best value because most people choose the bigger crabs. I'm sure that if we had softshell crabs in Spain, this would be the traditional way to prepare them.

In a small, deep saucepan, heat the olive oil to 350 degrees (measured with a candy thermometer). Using a pair of scissors, remove the eyes and mouth of 1 crab. Flip the crab over and cut off the apron at the bottom of the crab's belly. Flip the crab over again, lift up the points of the crab, and insert the scissors to snip out the lungs (they look like hairy little fingers). Rinse the crab well to clean it, and place it on paper towels to absorb any extra moisture. Season with salt and white pepper to taste. Repeat with the other crab.

Put the flour on a plate and coat both sides of the crabs in the flour. Shake off any excess flour. Dip the crabs in the beaten egg, and shake off any excess egg. Then dip them into the breadcrumbs.

When the oil reaches 350 degrees, place 1 crab in the oil, being careful not to let it splash. You'll see bubbles and hear the crackling of the frying. After 1 minute, turn the crab over. Fry for another minute, and remove it from the oil. Place the crab on paper towels to absorb any excess oil. Wait 30 seconds between batches to make sure the oil returns to 350 degrees, and repeat with the other crab. Flip each cooked crab onto its back and cut it in half lengthwise. It's important that you do this on the belly side so the crab keeps its shape. On each plate, stand the half crab on its cut end. Serve immediately, with a lemon wedge.

José's tips

If you don't want to clean the crabs yourself, you can probably get your fish supplier to dress them for you.

Rossejat
Pan-fried angel hair pasta with shrimp

Serves 4

1 cup Traditional Fish Stock (page 184)

3 tablespoons Spanish extra-virgin olive oil

2 ounces monkfish, cut into ³/₄-inch cubes

¹/₄ pound angel hair pasta, broken into 1-inch pieces

1 garlic clove, peeled and very finely chopped

3 tablespoons Sofrito (page 37)

Salt to taste

8 medium shrimp, peeled, deveined, and cut into ³/₄-inch pieces

¹/₄ cup Allioli (pages 20 and 22), for serving

All through Catalonia, and especially in Barcelona, there are many dishes that use pasta in one form or another. This dates back to the time when the Catalonians invaded northern Italy, and took home some Italian ingredients with them. You find great cannelloni stuffed with pork and covered with béchamel, and traditional soups with shell-shaped pasta. But *rossejat* is the most unusual Catalan pasta dish: nowhere else is pasta cooked in this way. In Washington, Pepa León—who is a designer, painter, and great friend—makes the best one I ever ate away from home. She makes her stock with shellfish, and the whole dish is incredibly flavorful.

Bring the stock to a boil in a small saucepan. Once it boils, reduce the heat and maintain it at a simmer.

In a paella pan or a medium flameproof casserole, heat 1 tablespoon of the olive oil over high heat. Add the monkfish and sear on all sides, about 2 minutes. Remove the fish and set it aside.

Reduce the heat to medium-low, and add the remaining 2 tablespoons of oil and the pasta. Pan-fry, stirring it continuously with a wooden spoon, until the pasta has a golden brown color, about 10 minutes. Be careful not to burn the pasta. Add the garlic and cook for 1 minute. Then add the *sofrito* and raise the heat to medium. Pour in the hot stock and add salt to taste.

Add the shrimp and the seared monkfish pieces, and stir with a wooden spoon. You'll see the pasta absorbing the liquid. Don't touch the pan anymore. Cook for 6 minutes, until the liquid has evaporated.

Remove the pan from the heat and let the *rossejat* rest for 3 minutes. Heat a salamander or broiler, and place the casserole underneath until the pasta on the surface starts to curl up and brown slightly. Remove, and serve immediately with the allioli on the side.

José's tips

If you can buy shrimp with the head on, peel the shrimp and add the head and the shells to the fish stock. Boil them together for 10 minutes to increase the flavor.

If you like crab, chop one into 6 small pieces and use it instead of the shrimp and the monkfish.

chicken

chapter 14

capitulo 14

Recipes

Mar y montaña de pollo con bogavante
Chicken with lobster

Pollastre amb samfaina
Traditional chicken stew with eggplant and
peppers, Catalan-style

Pollastre amb samfaina a la moderna
Chicken with samfaina in a modern way

Caldo de pollo
Chicken stock

Pollo con frutos secos
Chicken with dried fruit

Wine tips

Ctonia from the Emporda-Costa Brava
region (Garnacha Blanca grape)

Mas La Plana from the Penedes region
(Cabernet Sauvignon/Merlot/Cabernet
Franc grapes)

Jean Leon from the Penedes region
(Merlot grape)

Placet from the Rioja region
(Viura grape)

Cune "Viña Real Oro" from
the Rioja region (Tempranillo grape)

pollo

There are many restaurants in Spain that cook chickens on rotisseries as a kind of fast food. When you drive by, you can smell the roasting chicken in the air. Then there's the warmth of a good *caldo de pollo,* or chicken stock. It seems that almost every cookbook you read, no matter what country it's from, uses chicken stock in many recipes. This book is no different. But for me, the chicken I love best is an often-forgotten part of the bird: the oysters. Nowadays we're so used to seeing chicken in pieces—legs, thighs, breasts, livers—that the pleasures of the whole chicken are often overlooked. The oysters of the chicken fascinate me. You'll find them at the base of the chicken's back, on both sides, where the leg meets the spine. It's the juiciest, fattest piece of the chicken, and it's never sold separately in the supermarket. I pan-fry them quickly and devour them on my own.

Still, we face serious challenges with the chickens we often buy today. There's a Spanish saying that captures the blandness of the mass-produced chickens in countless supermarkets: *Este pollo no sabe como los de antes.* (This chicken doesn't taste like they used to.) Farm birds of all kinds used to have a darker meat and a richer taste than today's supermarket chicken. Now, happily, in Spain and in the United States, we are rediscovering why chickens used to be kept for Sundays and special occasions. Among the farmers at the hugely popular Dupont Circle market in Washington, D.C., is Bev Eggleston of EcoFriendly Foods, who has raised chickens the old way (in the open air, eating natural grains) at his farm in Virginia's Shenandoah Valley. Thanks to farmers like Bev, these new organic chickens can help us all re-create the taste of original Spanish dishes, such as *pollo con bogavante* (chicken and lobster).

Everyone thinks of surf and turf as the classic American combination, but in Catalan cooking, *pollo con bogavante* is an even better duo. The big difference is that we cook it as a stew, instead of laying the two foods next to each other on a plate. The flavors and textures of both ingredients become one in the classic *sofrito* sauce, proving that chicken (and not beef) is the perfect partner for anything from the sea.

José's tips

We cook the lobster apart from the chicken in order to preserve its flavor and texture. That's why it's very important to add the medallions right at the end of the cooking, or they will be overcooked. And remember to use the coral juices sparingly because they are strong—the essence of the lobster.

Mar y montaña de pollo con bogavante
Chicken with lobster

Serves 4

1 Maine lobster
(about 1½ pounds)

4 tablespoons Spanish
extra-virgin olive oil

4 chicken drumsticks

1 sprig fresh thyme

Salt to taste

Black pepper to taste

3 ounces fresh wild
mushrooms, preferably
morels, cleaned

½ tablespoon unsalted
butter

2 tablespoons Spanish
brandy

½ cup Sofrito (page 37)

2 cups Chicken Stock
(page 222)

2 tablespoons chopped
flat-leaf parsley

One of the main characteristics of Catalan cooking is pairing meat and seafood, especially in stews. Here is the perfect example—and the perfect combination of flavors and textures.

With a sharp knife and working over a large bowl, separate the lobster claws from the head; cut the head from the tail. Working along the segments, cut the tail into 4 medallions. Carefully crack the claws, taking care not to harm the meat.

Take the head and discard the membrane sac. Remove the gray coral, place in a blender, and process until smooth. Strain, and set aside. Cut what remains of the head into pieces and set aside with any juices.

Heat 1 tablespoon of the oil in a deep sauté pan over a medium-high flame. Add the drumsticks and thyme. Season with salt and pepper, and cook until brown on all sides, 8 minutes. Remove the chicken. Add 1 tablespoon of the oil and the mushrooms and sauté until golden, 2 minutes. Remove the mushrooms.

Add 1 tablespoon of the oil and the lobster medallions and claws. Sear on both sides, 2 minutes. Remove the lobster.

Add the remaining 1 tablespoon of oil and the butter with the reserved pieces of the lobster head and juices and sauté for 2 minutes. Using a wooden spoon, press the head into the pan to break up the shell.

Add the brandy and cook until reduced by one third, 30 seconds. Add the *sofrito* and cook for 1 minute. Pour in the stock and cook until the flavors merge thoroughly, 10 to 15 minutes; scoop off any foam that rises.

Pour the contents of the pan into a blender. Blend, strain, and return to the pan.

Add the chicken. Lower the heat to medium and cook until the chicken is done, 5 minutes. Add the lobster medallions, claws, and mushrooms. Heat until the lobster is warmed, about 2 minutes (don't overcook the lobster). Add salt to taste.

Remove the pan from the heat and stir in a little of the blended lobster coral to taste. Sprinkle with parsley, and serve.

Pollastre amb samfaina
Traditional chicken stew with eggplant and peppers, Catalan-style

Serves 4

5 ripe plum tomatoes

4 tablespoons Spanish extra-virgin olive oil

4 chicken thighs (about ¾ pound)

Salt to taste

Black pepper to taste

2 garlic cloves, peeled

1 Spanish onion, peeled and cut into 1-inch pieces

½ green bell pepper, seeded and cut into 1-inch pieces

½ red bell pepper, seeded and cut into 1-inch pieces

1 medium zucchini, cut into 1-inch cubes (about 1 cup)

1 medium eggplant, cut into 1-inch cubes (about 1 cup)

1 fresh bay leaf

3 sprigs fresh thyme

2 tablespoons chopped flat-leaf parsley

All across the Mediterranean, the mix of eggplant, tomatoes, and zucchini is incredibly popular and versatile. The chicken makes it a great tapa, especially when it is served with fried eggs.

Cut an X in the bottom of 3 of the tomatoes with a sharp knife. Fill a large bowl with very hot water, and blanch the tomatoes in the hot water for 10 seconds. Drain, and remove the skin and seeds. Cut the flesh into 1-inch pieces and place them in a bowl. Puree the other 2 tomatoes in a blender and strain the puree. Set the tomato pieces and puree aside.

Heat 2 tablespoons of the olive oil in a large sauté pan over a high flame. When the oil is hot, add the chicken thighs, skin side down, and brown on all sides, 2 to 3 minutes. Don't overcrowd the pan—you need space between the chicken pieces to brown them properly. Cook in batches if necessary. Season with salt and black pepper to taste and set the browned chicken aside.

Add the remaining 2 tablespoons of olive oil to the same pan, and lower the heat to medium. Split open the garlic cloves by placing them on a chopping board and pressing down hard on them with the base of your hand or with the flat side of a knife. Add the garlic to the pan and cook until golden, about 2 minutes. Add the onions and cook until they are soft and translucent, about 5 minutes. Add the bell peppers and cook for 4 minutes. Add the zucchini and cook for another 4 minutes. Add the eggplant and cook for 6 minutes.

Add the reserved tomato pieces and tomato puree, and cook until the tomato darkens in color, about 8 minutes.

Return the browned chicken to the pan and add the bay leaf and thyme. Cook for 10 minutes, or until the chicken is cooked through. Sprinkle with the parsley and serve immediately.

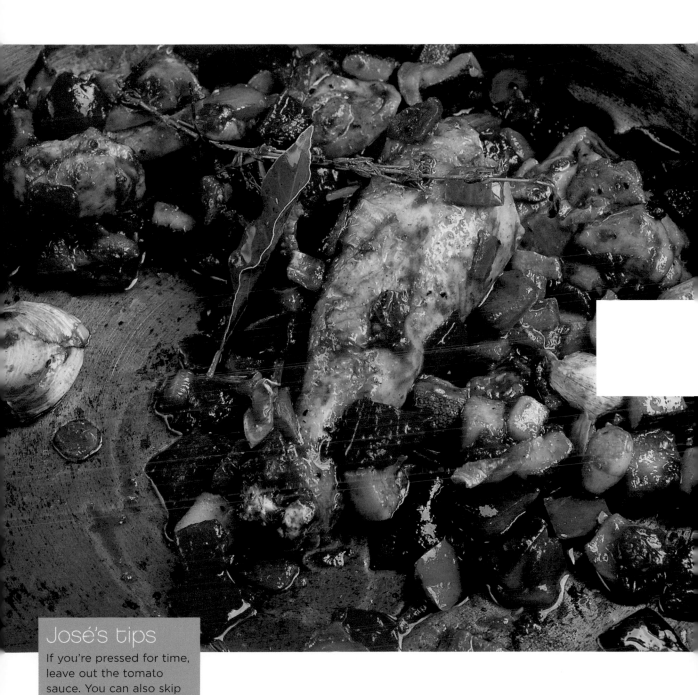

José's tips

If you're pressed for time, leave out the tomato sauce. You can also skip peeling and seeding the tomatoes when you make the tomato cubes.

Pollastre amb samfaina a la moderna
Chicken with samfaina in a modern way

Serves 4

3½ tablespoons Spanish extra-virgin olive oil

2 boneless chicken thighs, cut into ½-inch cubes

Salt to taste

¼ Spanish onion, peeled and cut into ¼-inch pieces (about ½ cup)

1 garlic clove, peeled and finely chopped

½ green bell pepper, seeded and cut into ¼-inch pieces (about ½ cup)

½ red bell pepper, seeded and cut into ¼-inch pieces (about ½ cup)

⅓ zucchini, cut into ¼-inch cubes (about ⅓ cup)

⅓ eggplant, peeled and cut into ¼-inch cubes (about ⅓ cup)

1 ripe plum tomato, cut into ¼-inch cubes (about ¼ cup)

Black pepper to taste

1 tablespoon chopped flat-leaf parsley

This is a quick version of the classic Catalan stew. It relies on meticulous cutting of the vegetables into cubes that are all the same size, to speed the cooking and create a perfect presentation. This tapa looks as good as it tastes.

Heat 1 tablespoon of the olive oil in a large sauté pan over a medium flame. Add the chicken cubes and sear them quickly on all sides, about 1 minute. Be careful not to overcrowd the pan, or the chicken will steam rather than sear. If necessary, cook the chicken in batches. Add salt and set the seared cubes aside.

In the same pan, heat ½ tablespoon of the oil over a medium flame. Add the onions and garlic and sauté for 2 minutes, stirring a little to make sure they brown evenly.

Raise the flame to high and add ½ tablespoon of the oil to the pan; then add the peppers and sauté for 2 minutes. Add ½ tablespoon more oil to the pan; add the zucchini and sauté for 3 minutes. Finally, add ½ tablespoon oil to the pan; add the eggplant and sauté for 3 minutes until the eggplant is soft. Transfer the vegetables to a bowl, add salt to taste, and set aside.

Add the remaining ½ tablespoon of oil and the tomatoes to the pan. Cook for 2 to 3 minutes. Return all the vegetables to the pan and sauté for 1 minute to reheat them.

Return the chicken to the pan and warm it for 20 seconds. Season with salt and pepper to taste, sprinkle with the parsley, and serve immediately.

José's tips

I'm a big fan of skin-on chicken when it's cooked to a nice golden brown color. But if you don't like it, you can remove it and then cut the chicken into cubes. You can also substitute any meat you want—pork, veal, beef, or even sausage—for the chicken. This tapa is incredibly versatile.

Caldo de pollo
Chicken stock

Makes about 2 quarts

1 chicken (about 2¹/₂ pounds;
see tips), rinsed

3 carrots, peeled

2 onions, peeled and halved

1 leek, well washed, outer
leaves removed

1 head garlic, papery outer
skin removed, halved

¹/₄ cup Spanish
extra-virgin olive oil

1 tablespoon black
peppercorns

1 bay leaf

1 sprig fresh thyme

10 sprigs fresh parsley

Salt to taste

I usually use a whole chicken to make my stock because my wife uses the chicken meat—a great by-product of making stock—for many dishes: in *croquetas* or mixed with mayonnaise for a salad. You can also just mix it with the stock to create a great chicken soup.

Put 4 quarts of water in a stockpot and add all the ingredients except the salt. Bring to a boil. As the stock comes to the boil, foam will form on the surface. Scoop this off immediately, so that your stock will end up as clear and clean as possible.

Reduce the heat to low and simmer for 2 hours. Add salt to taste, and remove from the heat. Strain the stock and store it in the refrigerator for up to 1 week or in the freezer until you need it.

José's tips

If you don't want to buy a whole chicken, you can always buy some parts—such as breasts, thighs, or drumsticks. Just make sure they have the bones inside them to flavor the stock.

José's tips
This dish also works great
with thinly sliced pork
tenderloin or leg of lamb.

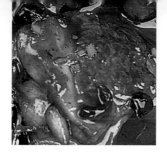

Pollo con frutos secos
Chicken with dried fruit

Serves 4

4 tablespoons Spanish extra-virgin olive oil

4 chicken tenders (about ½ pound)

Salt to taste

1 garlic clove

½ Spanish onion, peeled and cut into thin strips

8 dried apricots

2 dried prunes

1 tablespoon raisins

2 tablespoons hazelnuts, shelled and cut in half

1 tablespoon pine nuts

2 walnut halves, broken into ¼-inch pieces

1 cinnamon stick

2 tablespoons Spanish brandy

½ cup sweet wine, such as a Spanish Moscatel

1½ cups Chicken Stock (page 222)

1 teaspoon chopped chives

There are many recipes that feature the combination of dried fruits and meats. Usually these dishes are stews with long cooking times, and they make delicious meals. But in today's world, it's good to come up with alternatives that are fast-cooking yet still follow the tradition they come from. This tapa is great—a quick, modern recipe that draws on the Catalan tradition of cooking meats with dried fruits.

Heat 2 tablespoons of the olive oil in a medium sauté pan over a medium-high flame. Season the chicken tenders with salt to taste, and place them in the pan. Sear the chicken until golden brown, 2 minutes on each side. Remove and set aside.

Split open the garlic clove by placing it on a chopping board and pressing down hard on it with the base of your hand or with the flat side of a knife. Add the garlic to the sauté pan and cook over a medium flame for 30 seconds. Add the remaining 2 tablespoons of olive oil and the onions, and cook until the onions caramelize, around 10 minutes. If the onions start to get too brown, add ½ tablespoon of water to keep them cooking evenly.

Add the dried fruits, nuts, cinnamon stick, and brandy. Cook until the brandy is reduced by half, about 10 seconds. Add the sweet wine and reduce for 30 seconds.

Pour in the chicken stock, stir, and continue cooking until you have a nice sauce, about 3 minutes.

Return the browned chicken to the pan and cook for 30 seconds to heat it through. Sprinkle with the chives, and serve.

pork

chapter 15

capitulo 15

Recipes

Chorizo a la sidra
Asturian chorizo stewed in hard cider

Trucha con jamón
Trout with ham

Croquetas de jamón serrano y pollo
Serrano ham and chicken fritters

Butifarra amb mongetes del Ganxet "Daniel
Patrick Moynihan"
Catalan pork sausage with white beans

Solomillo asado con manzanas
Roasted pork tenderloin with apples

Higos con jamón
Figs with Spanish ham

Wine tips

Finca la Estacada "Seleccion Varietal" from the
Castilla la Mancha region (Tempranillo/Cabernet
Sauvignon grapes)

Marques de Vargas Reserva from the Rioja region
(Tempranillo grape)

L'alleu from the Montsant region
(Garnacha grape)

Pasanau from the Priorat region
(Garnacha/Cabernet Sauvignon grapes)

San Roman from the Toro region
(Tinta de Toro grape)

Hecula from the Yecla region
(Monastrel grape)

cerdo

On a high plateau surrounded by three mountains stands a town that holds the stuff of legend for Spanish gourmets. Guijuelo is not the prettiest town in the Salamanca region of central Spain; it's filled with industrial-looking warehouses. But its streets are also filled with signs beckoning visitors to places where they can eat its most famous product: *jamón ibérico de bellota,* the world's best ham. *Jamón ibérico* has three defining traits: it's made from wild Iberian pigs; those pigs are fed on a diet of acorns *(bellotas);* and the ham tastes extraordinarily good. As full-bodied as a fine Rioja and as rich as foie gras, Guijuelo's *jamón* is the caviar of hams.

Yet there's one sign you won't see among the *jamón* houses advertising themselves on the streets of Guijuelo. Opposite a residential building in a quiet corner of town, where people hang their washing in the street, there's a concrete building with shutters on the side. There's no sign on the front, nothing to tell you this is the home of Joselito, the best *jamón ibérico.* Inside, behind a couple of offices, a simple wooden door opens onto a dark, cavernous room filled with an overwhelming aroma of curing hams. Hanging on the walls and from the ceiling, several rows deep, are thousands of legs of ham with brown cards attached. Each card carries the name of the customer who bought the ham two years before it arrives at their table. Joselito needs no advertising: you're lucky if you can lay your hands on one of his hams.

In his kitchen two blocks away, José Gómez Martín, the owner of Joselito, explains what makes a great *jamón ibérico.* Each pig roams wild on two and a half acres of land, eating the acorns that give the hams such a distinctively rich and buttery flavor. From the Extremadura region in the southwest, where they are raised, the pigs travel north to Guijuelo to be butchered, salted, cured, and matured. But it's also the mountains around the town that are special. In the winter months, José opens the north-facing shutters of his warehouse to the cold mountain air to help the salting and drying process on the upper floor. In the summer, he opens the shutters on the southern side of the building to allow the hot summer air to cure the

hams. Finally, the precious hams sit downstairs in the dark until they are ready for the finest restaurants across Europe, two years later.

If it's hard to buy Joselito *jamón* in Spain, it's even harder in the United States. Until recently, government restrictions have been a huge barrier to Spain's cured meats; the traditional slaughtering techniques make such *jamón* impossible to import into the United States. That means Americans have been denied the very best *jamón,* although you can now buy some *jamón serrano,* its less illustrious relative. In the meantime, you can easily buy other pork products, including the classic chorizo sausage. And of course you can buy American pork and cook it in a Spanish way, as we do here. Hopefully, by the time you read this, Spain's ham makers will have convinced American officials to let their precious hams cross the Atlantic—so you too can eat *jamón ibérico.*

Chorizo a la sidra
Asturian chorizo stewed in hard cider

Serves 4

1 tablespoon Spanish
extra-virgin olive oil

4 semi-dry chorizo sausages
(each about 2 ounces;
see tips), cut into
1/2-inch-thick slices

1 cup hard cider

Crusty bread, for serving

In January 2004, *Food & Wine* magazine invited me to contribute to an article about my home region of Asturias. The idea was to follow me around this wonderful part of Spain, showing readers its gastronomical treasures. One of the recipes that I chose to illustrate the article was *chorizo a la sidra*. Pork and apples are, in many ways, the two classic ingredients of Asturian cooking. They also happen to be the perfect match for each other.

Heat the olive oil in a medium sauté pan over a medium flame. Place the chorizos in the pan and cook until they are slightly browned on all sides, about 5 minutes.

Pour the hard cider into the pan and raise the heat to high. Bring to a boil, then lower the heat to medium. Cook for around 30 minutes, until the chorizos are soft and the cider is reduced to about 2/3 cup.

Place a chorizo in each soup bowl and cover with the reduced cider. Serve with a hunk of crusty bread.

José's tips

As I've recommended elsewhere, it's worth taking the trouble to find a real Spanish chorizo.
If you can't locate a supplier, buy a fresh chorizo made with sweet paprika or *pimentón*.
It's not as good as the real thing, but it's okay as a substitute.

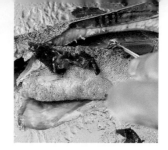

Trucha con jamón
Trout with ham

Serves 4

1 trout (about ½ pound;
see tips), boned

2 slices *jamón serrano*
(Spanish cured ham)

1 pinch of salt,
plus more to taste

1 tablespoon Spanish
extra-virgin olive oil

This is another example of Spanish cooking at its best: two main ingredients with minimal cooking. The ham adds saltiness to the fish, and the ham fat flavors the oil as the fish cooks.

Cut the head and tail off the trout, and discard both. Open the trout and place the ham inside. Season the inside and outside of the trout with the pinch of salt.

Heat the olive oil in a sauté pan over a medium flame. When the oil starts to smoke, place the trout in the pan and cook for 3 minutes. Using a spatula, carefully turn the fish over, and cook for 2 minutes on the other side.

Add salt to taste and cut the trout into 4 pieces. Serve immediately.

José's tips

If you can't find trout, look for monkfish; make two cuts in the side of the loin and insert the ham in them.

If you can't find a Spanish ham, a good piece of smoked bacon will serve as a good substitute. Just pan-fry the bacon a little before putting it inside the fish. You can then use the bacon fat along with the olive oil to cook the fish.

Croquetas de jamón serrano y pollo
Serrano ham and chicken fritters

Makes about 36 fritters

8 tablespoons (1 stick) unsalted butter

½ Spanish onion, peeled and finely chopped (about ½ cup)

2½ cups all-purpose flour

4 cups whole milk

½ cup finely chopped *jamón serrano* (Spanish cured ham)

6 ounces chicken, boiled and shredded (leftover chicken from making stock is ideal)

½ teaspoon salt

1 pinch nutmeg

2 large eggs, beaten

1 cup breadcrumbs

2 cups Spanish extra-virgin olive oil

I don't know anyone in Spain who doesn't love *croquetas,* and they are one of those dishes that always taste better at home. But today many tapas restaurants offer a huge variety of *croquetas,* filling them with different mixtures. At my Jaleo restaurants they are one of our most popular tapas, proving that good taste travels. When my daughter Carlota invited her entire class to Jaleo, it was the *croquetas* that her thirty classmates devoured.

Heat the butter in a medium sauté pan over a medium flame. Add the onions and cook until they are translucent, 5 minutes. Add 1½ cups of the flour and mix energetically. Cook for 5 minutes to make sure the flour is cooked through; it should start to take on a golden color. Pour the milk into the flour mixture and cook, stirring continuously, for about 2 minutes, until you have a thick béchamel.

Add the ham and chicken, and sprinkle in the salt and nutmeg. Cook for another 2 minutes. You should now have a thick mixture that you can mold in your hands. Carefully pick up a bit and try to ball it with your hands. It shouldn't be too sticky. If it does stick to your hands, cook it a little longer. Spread the mixture on a cookie sheet and let it cool to room temperature.

Take a spoonful of the cooled béchamel mixture and roll it in your hands to make a small cylinder the size of a wine cork. Roll the cylinder in the remaining 1 cup of flour, then in the eggs, and then in the breadcrumbs. Repeat with all the *croquetas.*

In a small, deep frying pan, heat the olive oil to 375 degrees (measured with a candy thermometer). Add the *croquetas* in small batches, making sure they are covered completely in oil. Fry until they have a nice golden color, about 1 minute; then transfer them to paper towels to drain. Repeat with all the *croquetas,* and serve hot.

José's tips

Croquetas are highly versatile, adaptable to whatever you have on hand. This recipe is a starting point. Instead of *jamón serrano* you can use more boiled chicken, boiled egg, or other types of ham if you like. You can even add leftover crab or shrimp.

Butifarra amb mongetes del Ganxet
"Daniel Patrick Moynihan"
Catalan pork sausage with white beans

Serves 4

1/4 pound dried white beans, such as navy beans

1 bay leaf

1/2 Spanish onion, peeled

1 carrot, peeled

6 tablespoons Spanish extra-virgin olive oil

Salt to taste

4 mild pork sausages (about 3/4 pound total)

2 garlic cloves, peeled and finely chopped

1 tablespoon chopped flat-leaf parsley

In 1993 a tall white-haired man with blue eyes started to come regularly to my tapas restaurant in downtown D.C. Every Sunday he was there at the door when we opened. The first thing he would order was a glass of white Muga Rioja and a plate of sausage and beans. Like a real Spaniard, he would go directly to the bar and eat standing up while he waited for his wife, Liz, or friends to join him. I must have spent hours talking with him about world affairs, including his meeting with the Spanish dictator Franco. I had no idea who he was, this distinguished man with the incredible stories. Two weeks after I first met him, I noticed that people were asking my new friend for his autograph. It was only then that I plucked up the courage to ask one of his friends for his name. Now when I think of this dish, I always remember Senator Daniel Patrick Moynihan. He might have celebrated his Irish roots, but to me his heart was really Spanish.

Place the beans in a bowl, cover with cold water, and soak overnight. The next day, drain and rinse them thoroughly.

Put the beans in a medium pot, cover with 1 1/2 quarts of water, and bring to a boil. Once the water begins to boil, add the bay leaf, onion, carrot, and 2 tablespoons of the olive oil. Reduce the heat to low and let the beans simmer slowly for 1 hour, periodically skimming off the foam that forms on the surface. Every 5 minutes or so, add a little cold water to slow down the boiling process. As the beans begin to soften, add salt to taste. When the beans are soft, scoop them out with a slotted spoon and set them aside.

Heat 3 tablespoons of the olive oil in a sauté pan over a medium flame. Add the sausages and cook until done, 8 to 10 minutes. Set them aside.

Add the remaining 1 tablespoon of olive oil to the same sauté pan. Add the garlic and sauté over a medium-high flame until it turns a light brown color, about 30 seconds. Add the beans and cook for 2 minutes. Add salt to taste.

Spoon a bed of beans onto a serving dish, and place the sausages on top. Sprinkle with the parsley, and serve.

José's tips

To make the dish traditionally, I recommend a mild pork sausage. You can find many different kinds in American supermarkets today.

If you don't want to go through the process of soaking and boiling the beans, use good-quality canned cooked beans from the supermarket.

Solomillo asado con manzanas
Roasted pork tenderloin with apples

Serves 4

1 pork tenderloin (1/2 pound)

1 tablespoon unsalted butter

2 tablespoons Spanish extra-virgin olive oil

1 Golden Delicious apple, peeled, cored, and cut into 8 pieces

1 white onion, peeled and thinly sliced

5 sprigs fresh oregano

1/4 teaspoon salt

1/4 teaspoon black pepper

2 tablespoons Spanish brandy

1/2 cup Chicken Stock (page 222)

More often than not, meats roasted in the oven are very gray on the outside while they're still pink inside. That's because we tend to cook meat at too high a temperature. The result: the first couple of inches on the outside are overcooked and dehydrated. What we should do is lower the heat. Cooking it at a lower temperature for a longer period of time allows for the gelatinization of all the meat, without letting it lose its juices. The future of cooking meat is one in which the thermometer will be king.

Heat the oven to 250 degrees.

Cut off and discard the ends of the tenderloin. Cut the tenderloin in half.

In a large ovenproof sauté pan, heat the butter and olive oil over a medium flame. Add the apple pieces and cook until they start to become soft and browned, 8 to 10 minutes. Remove the apples from the pan and set them aside.

Add the onions to the pan and cook until they start to brown, 4 to 5 minutes. Return the apples to the pan and cover them with the oregano sprigs.

Season the tenderloin with salt and pepper, and place the meat on top of the apples. Tilt the pan slightly and spoon a little of the oil-butter mixture over the pork. Put the sauté pan in the oven.

Cook the pork until the temperature at the heart of the tenderloin reaches 140 degrees, 25 to 30 minutes. (Turn the tenderloin after 10 minutes.) Remove it from the oven. Remove the pork from the sauté pan and wrap it in aluminum foil to keep warm.

Place the sauté pan over medium heat, add the brandy, and cook until reduced by half, about 1 minute. Then add the chicken stock and cook until it thickens slightly, forming a sauce, about 2 minutes.

Slice each piece of pork tenderloin in half. Spoon a little sauce onto each plate, and place a piece of pork on top. Add 2 pieces of apple on top, and serve hot.

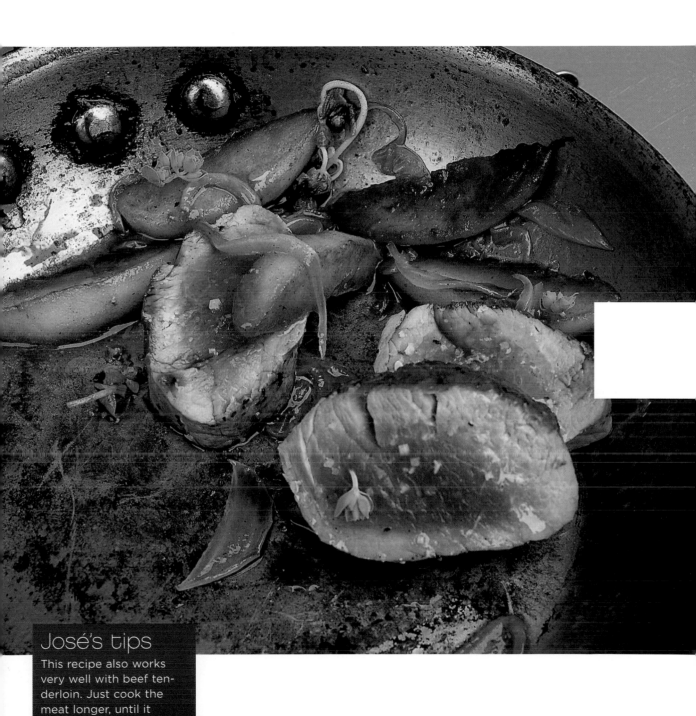

José's tips

This recipe also works very well with beef tenderloin. Just cook the meat longer, until it reaches 140 degrees inside.

José's tips

Jamón serrano partners well with many fruits, including melon, pineapple, and the figs used here. Why? Because the saltiness of the ham and the sweetness of the fruit make an irresistible combination. If you don't have the time to peel and sear the figs, try quartering them and serving them raw with the ham and dressing.

Higos con jamón
Figs with Spanish ham

Serves 4

8 fresh black Mission figs

3 tablespoons Spanish extra-virgin olive oil

4 slices *jamón serrano* (Spanish cured ham), cut into 2-inch squares

2 teaspoons sherry vinegar

1 tablespoon herb flowers (chives or thyme, for instance), optional, for garnish

In Spain we are crazy for ham, and we have a few dishes that pair the natural saltiness of ham with the sweetness of fruit, such as melon or dates. For me, these figs are the perfect match (although quite frankly a very good Spanish ham doesn't really need any accompaniment). In summer, a very cold melon or figs topped with Spanish ham is one of the most refreshing dishes you will ever eat. I still remember my first Feria de Algeciras, the annual festival in the town my wife comes from. We were invited to a *caseta,* or private club, where they had a terrific *jamón ibérico* topped with very cold slices of melon. In the version below, I pair the ham with figs because they are my favorite fruit. They also bring back child-hood memories of picking them from the wild trees in Santa Coloma de Cervelló, near Barcelona.

Using a paring knife, carefully peel the figs (this is far easier to do when the figs are firm).

Heat 1 tablespoon of the olive oil in a nonstick pan over a high flame. Sear the figs for 20 seconds all over, then put them on a serving dish. Lay a square of *jamón serrano* on top of each fig.

Whisk the remaining 2 tablespoons oil with the vinegar in a small bowl, and drizzle around the plate. Garnish with the herb flowers (if using), and serve.

other
meats

chapter 16

capitulo 16

Recipes

Costillas de cordero con allioli de miel
Rack of lamb with honey allioli

Albóndigas con melocotones
Meatballs with peaches

Conejo con cerezas Santa Coloma de Cervelló
Rabbit with cherries

Wine tips

Cirsion From the Rioja region
(Tempranillo grape)

Mauro From the Castilla y Leon region
(Tempranillo grape)

Cervoles From the Costers del Segre region
(Cabernet Sauvignon/Garnacha grapes)

otras carnes

Every year, when it's open season in Spain, hunters gather in the fields to search for rabbits, or quail, or pheasants. My grandfather Ramón Puerta was one of those great Spanish hunters, and I vividly remember going hunting with him as a young child. I can still smell the leather belts full of ammunition and the gunshot in the air, and I can see the rituals of the hunt: waking up early, dressing in special pants, cleaning the guns. The hunter's clothes are sometimes passed from generation to generation, and my mother preciously keeps all the tools that my grandfather used to make his own cartridges. He died when I was just six years old, but I can still see his two hunting dogs and remember his tales of shooting and fishing in the mountains of Asturias. On one expedition, he spent two or three days in a mountain cabin with a group of friends. Each day, one of the hunters would stay behind to prepare the food for the others. My grandfather never cooked, but on one occasion he tried to cook rice with the pheasants and quail they'd caught. He filled up an entire casserole of raw rice, not knowing that it doubles or triples in volume during cooking. Of course the rice started to bubble up and overflow. Soon it was everywhere, and the only thing he could use to scoop it up was some terra-cotta tiles from the cabin roof. When his friends returned from the hunt, they were astonished. "Ramón, how much rice did you cook?" they asked. "Look outside," he replied. "There's even more out there."

It's not just my family. The traditions of hunting and country food are essential parts of Spanish cooking. One of Spain's national treasures, at least in the restaurant world, is the *asador,* or roasting house. In central Spain, where they raise lambs, one of the most popular dishes is a six-week-old baby lamb roasted on an *asador*'s wood-burning grill. It's right around the Duero river, where they produce one of the best wines in the world, Ribera del Duero—the perfect match for the smoky flavor of the roasted lamb. Every *asador* either raises its own lambs or has a special relationship with a farm where they know the lambs, what they eat, and how they live. It's that traditional connection to the land that gives Spanish cooking its vitality.

Here in Washington, I've tried to build my own relationships with local farmers and the countryside that gives us so much. We buy our baby lambs and fresh rabbits from a farmer in the Appalachian hills of Fulton County, Pennsylvania. There, among the white clapboard homes and steepled churches that remind me so much of Aaron Copland's music, Don Lake raises rabbits in his garden and lambs on his farm. It feels a lot like Asturias to me: a hilly region, where everyone seems to be a small farmer, raising chickens in their yard or growing vegetables to eat and sell.

It often seems that the only meats available in supermarkets are chicken, beef, and pork. But the truth, as Don knows, is that the world of meats doesn't end there. If you dig around in your supermarket, or find a good butcher at a local market, you can rediscover the forgotten pleasures of a rabbit stew, or a roasted lamb, or a juicy quail.

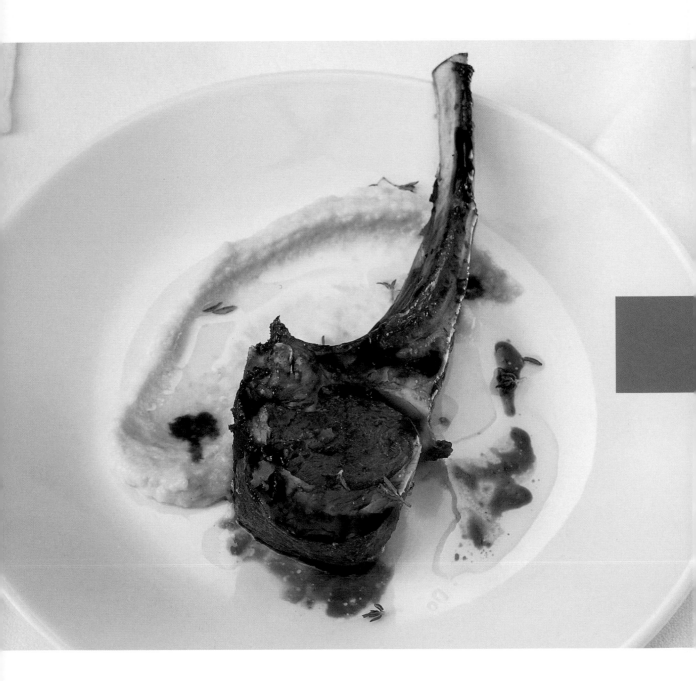

Costillas de cordero con allioli de miel
Rack of lamb with honey allioli

Serves 4

1 rack of lamb
(about 1 pound)

1 sprig fresh rosemary

1 tablespoon Spanish extra-
virgin olive oil, plus extra for
brushing the meat

½ cup Allioli
(pages 20 and 22)

2 tablespoons lavender
honey (or any other honey
you like)

Salt to taste

Allioli is the national sauce of Catalonia—it accompanies practically any grilled meat. Catalans also have a sweet tooth, which you find in traditional recipes like codfish with honey, or meats cooked with fruits. Honey *allioli* is a traditional combination that goes perfectly with lamb. Even with its garlic flavor, you'll find this dish is popular with kids, too.

Heat the oven to 250 degrees.

Using a sharp knife, remove the fat from the rack of lamb so the bones are clean but still attached to the loin.

Place the lamb, with the bones facing down, on a roasting rack or directly in a roasting pan. Break the sprig of rosemary into a few pieces and sprinkle them over the lamb. Brush the lamb with a little olive oil. Roast for 30 minutes, or until the interior of the meat reaches 130 degrees. While it is cooking, baste the meat once or twice with a little oil from the pan.

Meanwhile, combine the *allioli* and the honey in a bowl. Use a fork to mix them together thoroughly.

Remove the lamb from the oven and allow it to rest for 3 or 4 minutes.

Heat the 1 tablespoon of olive oil in a large sauté pan over a high flame. Place the whole rack of lamb in the pan and sear for 10 seconds on each side to brown it.

Cut the rack into pieces along the bones. Place a spoonful of honey *allioli* on each plate, and top with a piece of lamb. Sprinkle with salt to taste, and serve.

José's tips

We sear the lamb at the end, not the beginning, because we want to achieve the Maillard reaction. What's that? I don't want to get too deep, but it's what happens every time we brown meats that are rich in sugar. By roasting the lamb slowly, we lose much less juice than during traditional roasting at high heats. And by searing it at the end, we can also conserve more of the lamb's succulent juices.

Albóndigas con melocotones
Meatballs with peaches

Serves 4

For the meatballs

¹/₂ ounce (about ¹/₂ slice)
stale white bread

2 tablespoons whole milk

¹/₄ pound ground beef
(coarsely ground)

1 garlic clove, peeled and
finely chopped

2 tablespoons very finely
chopped parsley

1 tablespoon beaten egg

1 teaspoon salt

2 tablespoons
all-purpose flour

¹/₄ cup Spanish
extra-virgin olive oil

For the sauce and fruit

2 teaspoons pine nuts

1 tablespoon sugar

2 tablespoons unsalted
butter

1 ripe, medium-size peach,
peeled, halved, pitted, and
sliced into 12 segments

2 tablespoons sherry vinegar

1¹/₂ cups Chicken Stock
(page 222)

1 cinnamon stick

1 tablespoon finely
chopped parsley

I have to admit I have a taste for sweet things. While I was not born in Catalonia, I grew up there and was fascinated by the many regional dishes that mix fresh or dried fruits with meats. I was inspired to create this meat and fruit pairing by the wonderful peaches I've bought at my local farmers' market at Dupont Circle in Washington, D.C. It evokes the best of this wonderful Catalan combination.

Prepare the meatballs: Place the bread in a small bowl and pour the milk over it, using just enough milk to soften the bread. Let it sit for 1 minute.

In a large mixing bowl, combine the ground beef, milk-soaked bread, garlic, parsley, and egg. Using a spoon, mix all the ingredients together. Add the salt, and continue mixing. Place the flour on a plate. Form 1-inch balls of the meat mixture (you should end up with 12 meatballs), and roll them in the flour. Shake off any excess flour, and set the meatballs aside. Heat the olive oil in a medium saucepan over a medium flame. When the oil reaches 350 degrees (measured with a candy thermometer), add the meatballs in small batches. Pan-fry until brown all over, about 4 minutes. Set the meatballs aside on paper towels to drain.

Make the sauce: In a small sauté pan, toast the pine nuts over medium-low heat, stirring regularly to ensure they don't burn, until they turn light brown, 3 minutes. Remove the pine nuts from the pan and set aside.

Place a large sauté pan over low heat, add the sugar, and cook until golden, about 2 minutes. Stir the butter into the sugar and allow it to melt. Then add the peach slices and sauté until they are brown on all sides, about 2 minutes. Remove the peaches and set them aside. Add the vinegar and cook until reduced by half, about 1 minute. Add the stock, reserved pine nuts, and the cinnamon stick. Cook until the sauce starts to thicken, about 3 minutes.

Add the meatballs to the pan. Bring the sauce to a boil and then reduce the heat to a simmer. Cook for 5 minutes, moving the pan constantly to ensure that the meatballs cook evenly. The sauce should end up being thick and syrupy. Return the peach slices to the pan to heat through. Sprinkle with the parsley, and serve immediately.

José's tips
You can use any meat you like for this dish. You can also substitute apricots for the peaches, or use dried apricots at any time of year.

Conejo con cerezas Santa Coloma de Cervellò
Rabbit with cherries

Serves 4

½ medium rabbit, preferably a front quarter (about 1 pound), cut into 8 pieces

¼ teaspoon salt, plus more to taste

2 garlic cloves

3 tablespoons Spanish extra-virgin olive oil

1 Spanish onion, peeled and thinly sliced

18 fresh cherries, pitted and halved

½ cup sweet wine, such as sherry or moscatel

2 cups Chicken Stock (page 222)

1 cinnamon stick

Salt to taste

Santa Coloma de Cervellò is very close to my heart because it's the town where I grew up. From my bedroom window I could see the orchards and the blanket of pink cherry blossoms each spring. (Maybe that's one reason why I love living in Washington, D.C., with its breathtaking cherry blossoms.) I remember spending hours after school among the trees, stuffing my face with cherries. They were dangerous pickings, too, with the shotgun-toting farmer looking out for us. To this day, the cherries of Santa Coloma de Cervellò remain the best I've ever tasted. When I was just fourteen, I collected recipes in a tiny book that the town council printed. Among them was a dish of rabbit with cherries, not so different from the recipe here.

Sprinkle the rabbit with ¼ teaspoon salt. Split open the garlic cloves by placing them on a chopping board and pressing down hard with the base of your hand or with the flat side of a knife. Heat 2 tablespoons of the oil in a large pan over a high flame. Add the rabbit and brown, about 4 minutes on each side; you want to brown the outside quickly, without drying the inside. Remove the rabbit pieces and set aside.

Reduce the heat to medium-low and add the remaining 1 tablespoon of oil to the pan. Sauté the garlic for 1 minute. Add the onions and 6 of the cherries. Cook until the onions are caramelized and soft, around 20 minutes. Be careful not to burn the onions. If they start to get too dark, add 1 tablespoon of water.

Once the onions are soft and brown, raise the heat to high and add the sweet wine. Cook until the wine has evaporated, 2 minutes. Add 1 cup of the stock and transfer to a blender. Blend thoroughly, strain, and return to the pan. Return the rabbit to the pan and heat over a low flame. Add the cinnamon and the remaining stock, and cook slowly for 10 to 15 minutes. Add salt to taste.

Place the remaining 12 cherries in the pan and cook gently for 5 minutes. (Don't overcook the cherries or they'll fall apart and lose their freshness.) Serve immediately.

José's tips

You'll have to buy a whole rabbit, so you can either save the rest for another recipe or cook the whole rabbit and make this a main course.

sources

With more and more Americans discovering Spain and its wonderful culinary heritage, consumers have begun to seek out Spanish products to try at home. Many food markets and specialty stores across the country have started carrying Spanish olive oils, cheeses, hams, sausages, and more. Ask your grocer or check out these sources.

Amigo Foods

Amigo Foods carries some Spanish cheeses, *embutidos* (dry-cured meats), and other Spanish products. www.amigofoods.com

Dean & Deluca

At many of their locations, Dean & Deluca offers a pretty good selection of Spanish cheeses such as Garotxa and Majorero, along with *jamón serrano*, chorizo sausage, piquillo peppers, Spanish saffron, tuna, capers, olives, anchovies, and chocolate. www.deananddeluca.com

Despana Brand Foods

They carry meats, *jamón serrano*, cheeses, cookware, spices, and more from Spain. They have a website, www.despanabrandfoods.com, but you'll need to e-mail or phone in your order.

José Andrés Gourmet products

Along with recipes and regular updates, my website is a great resource for Spanish travel and food. www.joseandres.com

La Española

At this online store you can find a huge assortment of *embutidos* (dry-cured meats) and cheeses. They carry *compango Asturiano*, an assortment of *jamón*, bacon, chorizo, and *morcilla* (blood sausage) that is used to make *Fabada Asturiana*. www.laespanola.com

The Spanish Table

This online store carries Spanish cheeses, *embutidos*, olive oils, and other products. www.spanishtable.com

La Tienda

This online store offers a wide variety of Spanish foods, including *jamón serrano*, chorizo sausage, piquillo peppers, saffron, tuna, capers, olives, anchovies, chocolate, and cheeses such as Idiazábal and Manchego. www.tienda.com

Wegmans

This Rochester-based company's stores carry Spanish olive oil, piquillo peppers, Spanish saffron, tuna, capers, olives, anchovies, chocolate, *pimentón*, Spanish cheeses, chickpeas and beans, bomba rice, and more. www.wegmans.com

Whole Foods

Many Whole Foods stores carry items like Spanish saffron, tuna, and anchovies. The cheese counter often stocks cheeses such as Valdeón, Idiazábal, Manchego, and more—even the hard-to-find Torta del Casar. www.wholefoodsmarket.com

Zingerman's

This Ann Arbor–based store carries some Spanish cheeses as well as *membrillo* (quince compote) and other Spanish products. Available by catalog or at www.zingermans.com

acknowledgments

Finally I have a book. And I'm not so sure I want another one. But what I learned from this book is the true meaning of teamwork and friendship. It has many faces: many people who either directly or indirectly are a big part of every page—and each other's lives.

Richard Wolffe: If he hadn't written the first proposal, we wouldn't be here today. I wrote this book between naps, and sometimes while snoring, at his house and mine. Thank you for waking me up when we were supposed to be working. But best of all, thank you for being my best friend and for staying on the road with me to true friendship. Gracias especially to Paula Cuello, for sharing her half-orange.

Francesc Guillamet: For his passion, his creativity, and for waiting for the clouds to pass for the right light on every photo. Francesc works for love, not money, and it shows. And also thanks to Maribel Ruiz de Erenchun.

My burner team: Katsuya Fukushima, for always being there, for his smile and for his jackets; Ruben Garcia, for being my rock at the moment I needed it most; Rodolfo Guzman, for being by my side for more than twelve years; Steve Klc, pastry chef extraordinaire; Laura Trevino, for organizing my life and still staying happy somehow. For all their help over the years as well as their recipe-testing: Jorge Chicas, Terri Cutrino, John Paul Damato, Saul Herrera, Oscar Garcia, Secundino Gonzalez, Nicolas Guardado, Lauren Jones, Alex Mejia, Edgar Steele, Josh Whigham, Brandon Williams and Samantha Withall. And to everyone who has helped me move the restaurants forward.

My dining room team: Tony Yelamos, for his hard work and support; Maria Chicas, for all her work and her contagious smile; Christopher Vasquez, for always being there for me and for choosing the right flowers; Jimmy Pumarol; Manny Flores; Sandy Lewis; Joanna Brady. Thanks especially to Francisco Astudillo for choosing all the wines, and for his amazing nose.

My partners, Roberto Alvarez and Rob Wilder: for so many years of friendship and support, and for building me a stage to perform on.

Heather Freeman: She's the big sister I never had. Thanks for everything you do, all the time, to show the world my best side. Thanks also to Scott Homstead for supporting both of us so much.

Chris Pavone: For being a guiding force, and for adding the necessary salt to this book. And to Pam Krauss and the entire team at Clarkson Potter, for knocking this book into shape.

Kris Dahl at ICM: For playing the role of Charlie in my life. Thanks for making this book happen. Without you, a great idea would still be cooking in the pot.

Roberto Sablayrolles at Tasty Concepts: For being a great friend and for bringing these words to life with his remarkable design. Also a big thanks to his team, Daniel Troconis.

For sharing with me their experience of cookbooks: Rick Tramonto, Claudia Fleming, Bob Kinkead and Tom Colicchio. To all the writers who inspired me and opened the door to Spanish cookbooks in America, especially Coleman Andrews and Penelope Casas. To all the people who paved the way for Spanish cooking in America: especially Julian Serrano, Gabino Sotelino, Rufino Lopez, Paco Peña, Josu Zubikarai, and above all Clemente Bocos and Yolanda.

I can't thank enough all the many people who have written about Spanish food and wine and helped to bring it to the wider world. Thanks above all to Michael and Arianne Batterberry, who are my gastronomic parents in America and always believed in me; Phyllis Richman, who saw my future as a cook so early; Nikki and Michael Singer, for being true friends and visionaries, and for driving to Roses.

Who says the public and the private sector don't work well together? Thanks to all the people at ICEX in New York for their continued support over so many years, especially Luis de Velasco, Katrin Naelepa, Jeffrey Shaw, Sonia Ortega. To Jose Guerra, who always is ready and willing to help anyone in need, especially me. And to Pilar Vico from the Spanish tourist office, who has always been my biggest cheerleader.

To all the food and wine importers who help chefs like me get the best Spain has to offer: especially José Arcas, Aurelio Cabestrero, Almudena de Llaguno and Steve Metzer, Hugo Linares, Jorge Ordoñez and Miguel Puig.

A heartfelt thank-you to the wonderful community of chefs, restaurateurs and food writers in Washington who have always made me feel at home.

To all my friends in the food and restaurant community in Spain: You have inspired me and taught me everything I know. Ferran Adrià and Juli Soler: for being an eternally unselfish source of inspiration and guidance, and for opening their doors once again—this time for the photos in this book. Alberto Adrià: the best *cocinero* I know, for being a true friend who's always there with his insight and help. Thanks for being who you are. And thanks also to Silvia Perez for always taking my calls for help. Thanks to everyone, past and present, who is part of that amazing family known as el Bulli.

To all those who shared their culinary expertise with me through the years, especially Josep Puig, Jean-Louis Neichel, Tomas Herranz and Lluis Cruaynes.

Javier Canovas and Elena: *por ayudarme a encontrar un camino y mas.*

To my father, Marian, and my mother, Marisa, for planting the seed of my love for cooking. And to my brothers, Mariano, Jordi, and Eduardo, for great childhood memories. And to all my family in Spain for being a precious part of my life.

Restaurants, books, TV shows—nothing matters more than my family. Happiness isn't destiny, it's the road I travel every day with Tichi. Thank you for always steering me in the right direction, and for making the best gazpacho in the world. To my girls—Carlota, Ines and Lucia—I only have to see your joy cooking with me at home and devouring *croquetas* at the restaurants to know the true meaning of being a father.

—JA

I promised myself I wouldn't cowrite another book, but there's something about José Andrés that's irresistible. In public and private he's the same: big-hearted, funny, incredibly generous and exceptionally creative. He fills a room with his energy, and he's filled my life with his friendship over the last seven years. José—thank you for teaching me about Spain and about food, for taking my cooking to another dimension, and for being my best friend. An even bigger thank you to Tichi and the girls for sharing José with me (and the rest of the world), and for helping to make Washington our home.

Thanks is still far too small a word for Paula. This book was written at night and on weekends, in the middle of another presidential campaign, when I should have been supporting her. Instead, as always, she was supporting me and our three wonderful monkeys: Ilana, Ben, and Max. I can't thank her enough for her life and her love, her spirit and her inspiration. She's all states, and all princes I; Nothing else is.

—RW

index